To Dick,

I've enjoyed your stories and the feedback in recent years. I mention you often to mutual friends.

Best wishes,
Jim O'Brien
11-28-2012

WITH LOVE AND PRIDE

Portraits of a Pittsburgh Family

Stories and Photos
By Jim O'Brien

Books By Jim O'Brien

COMPLETE HANDBOOK OF PRO BASKETBALL 1970-1971

COMPLETE HANDBOOK OF PRO BASKETBALL 1971-1972

ABA ALL-STARS

PITTSBURGH: THE STORY OF THE CITY OF CHAMPIONS

HAIL TO PITT: A SPORTS HISTORY OF
THE UNIVERSITY OF PITTSBURGH

DOING IT RIGHT

WHATEVER IT TAKES

MAZ AND THE '60 BUCS

REMEMBER ROBERTO

PENGUIN PROFILES

DARE TO DREAM

KEEP THE FAITH

WE HAD 'EM ALL THE WAY

HOMETOWN HEROES

GLORY YEARS

THE CHIEF

STEELERS FOREVER

ALWAYS A STEELER

WITH LOVE AND PRIDE

LAMBERT: THE MAN IN THE MIDDLE

To order copies of these titles directly from the publisher, send $26.95 for hardcover edition. Please send $3.50 to cover shipping and handling costs per book. Pennsylvania residents add 6% sales tax to price of book only. Allegheny County residents add an additional 1% sales tax for a total of 7% sales tax. Copies will be signed by author at your request. Discounts available for large orders. Contact publisher regarding availability and prices of all books in Pittsburgh Proud series, or to request an order form. Some books are sold out and no longer available. You can still order the following: Doing It Right, Remember Roberto, We Had 'Em All The Way, Hometown Heroes, Glory Years, Keep The Faith, The Chief, Steelers Forever and Always a Steeler.

This book is dedicated to the memory of
my mother and father, Mary and Dan O'Brien,
and to my wife Kathie's mother and father,
Barbara and Harvey Churchman,
and to their grandchildren, Sarah and Rebecca.

Cover photo by Jim O'Brien

Editorial Assistance by Gerry Hamilton

Copyright © 2004 by Jim O'Brien

James P. O'Brien — Publishing
P.O. Box 12580
Pittsburgh PA 15241
Phone: (412) 221-3580

First printing: August, 2004

Manufactured in the United States of America

Printed by Geyer Printing Company, Inc.
3700 Bigelow Boulevard
Pittsburgh PA 15213

Typography by Cold-Comp
91 Green Glen Drive
Pittsburgh PA 15227

ISBN 1-886348-10-3

Introduction

It was the fall of 1980 and I was reporting for the second straight season on the Pittsburgh Steelers for *The Pittsburgh Press*. One sunny Saturday in September, I took my daughters, Sarah, 7, and Rebecca, 3½, with me to Three Rivers Stadium. Many of the players brought their children to Saturday practices. It was okay to do so.

Sarah and Rebecca met Art Rooney, the owner of the Steelers, and the nicest man I ever knew in sports. He was wearing a dark topcoat, a tweed cap and sunglasses. He posed for pictures with the girls. He couldn't have been nicer to them, treating them like they were his own grandchildren.

That same day, just as we were coming out of a tunnel onto the field, L.C. Greenwood sneaked up on us, and jumped out from behind a wall just as we were passing. He cried, "Boo!" Both of the girls screamed, and squirmed inside of my legs. They were holding onto me for dear life.

Keep in mind that L.C. Greenwood was a member of the Steelers' vaunted Steel Curtain. He was the tallest man on the team, at 6-feet-6½-inches. He was wearing his helmet and it had a hard plastic face shield that was dark tinted, similar to the mask worn by Darth Vader of "Star Wars" fame. So he scared them pretty good. Hell, he scared me.

The girls thought I could protect them. Goodness knows, I've tried. L.C. didn't mean to frighten them as much as he did, and so he felt badly about what he did. He started apologizing to them and being as friendly as Art Rooney. He ended up being one of their favorite players.

I took Sarah with me the following summer to the Steelers' training camp where she shared my room at Bonaventure Hall, where the players and media stayed in those days. At practice the next day, Ed Kiely, one of the team's public relations directors, came out of nowhere and placed a Steelers' ballcap on her head. Joe Greene and Rocky Bleier both came over and said hello to her in the dining hall. They would become favorites as well, along with Terry Bradshaw and Lynn Swann.

The next morning, Sarah and I stopped for breakfast at a Howard Johnson's on Route 51 on the way home. I asked her what she liked best about her stay at the Steelers' training camp. She looked me straight in the eyes and said, "Having you all to myself." It was a magic moment.

There have been lots of magic moments and mystifying moments in my interaction with my wife Kathie and our daughters, Sarah and Rebecca. We have had some special times with Kathie's parents, Barbara and Harvey Churchman, and my mother, Mary O'Brien. My dad, Dan O'Brien, died within two years of our wedding date, so he didn't figure much in our family life.

I've never kept a diary, but I had the good fortune of being able to write about my family, and the stuff that happens to families, in my weekly column. I was first approached about writing a column for *The Almanac* that goes into 65,000 homes in the South Hills of Pittsburgh by the publisher, Richard Barnes, back in 1990. Debbie Popp has been the managing editor all along, even after the *Observer-Reporter* bought the paper. Somewhere along the way, I also started writing a column for *The Valley Mirror*, first for Earle Wittpen and then for Tony Munson. They've allowed me to write about whatever struck my fancy.

I was determined to write a positive piece as often as possible. I choose subjects I thought affected all families. In one two-year period, for instance, Kathie and I lost her parents and my mother. It was a difficult time. Kathie broke her wrist somewhere in there. The events of September 11, 2001 happened after Kathie's parents had died and when my mother's mind had gone bad. My mother had no comprehension of the enormity of the catastrophe, or the death of

Steelers' owner Art Rooney poses with O'Briens at Three Rivers Stadium in 1980.

her sister Mildred Clark around the same time. I wrote about that, too.

Everybody had a personal story that related to 9/11. Kathie and I, for instance, had lunch one day at the Windows of the World Restaurant atop one of the World Trade towers. Kathie didn't know it at the time, but she was pregnant with Rebecca that day. She felt ill after lunch and had no idea why. Over 25 years later, when the World Trade Towers tumbled to earth after being struck by jet airplanes piloted by terrorists it hit home even more with us.

Such incidents and many much more minor happenings were the stuff that I wrote about. I always liked it when somebody told me one of my columns hit home with them, or that they'd had a similar experience, or that it helped them deal with the difficulty of looking after a mother whose mental or physical welfare was affected by old age. Kathie and I became grandparents as I was putting this book together. Margaret Harvey Zirwas, who is to be called Maggie, is the daughter of our Sarah and her husband, Matt Zirwas. This is a new chapter in our lives.

I have always written these columns as if I was writing to my best friend. I was simply telling the reader about something that happened that I had some thoughts about and that I wanted to share with them. This book is a collection of many of those personal stories. The photos are mine as well. I have been signing my books in recent years with the closing line "with love and pride." Thus the title for this book. I hope it hits home with you.

I don't have all the answers. I ask a lot of questions. I am still seeking the answers. I love my family and I am proud of my family. I hope they feel the same way about me. Holding Maggie's warm cheek against my cheek is the greatest feeling in the world, and it reminds me of the days when my girls were babies. Memories are so important to all of us.

Starting off on Sunnyside Street

April 4, 1990

I grew up on the shady street of Sunnyside Street. We had made a big move when I was about five years old, from 5413 Sunnyside Street, where my dad had been born about 40 years earlier — right on the living room couch — to 5410 Sunnyside Street where I spent the next 15 or 16 years.

This was in the Glenwood section of Pittsburgh, often referrred to as Hazelwood in the daily newspapers, especially when someone gets killed in the community. It was just a few blocks north of the Monongahela River, the Baltimore & Ohio Railroad yard, and the Pittsburgh Railways Company's so-called car barn. My grandparents worked at both places, so we were transportation moguls. Grandfather O'Brien was a streetcar motorman, and Grandfather Burns was the yardmaster at the B&O's Glenwood Yards. My dad also worked at the B&O, dropping out of school at age 15 to take a job. He later worked for over 35 years across the river at Mesta Machine Co. in West Homestead.

It was during my stay on Sunnyside Street that I became a sports writer, a sports commissioner, a promoter, a pain in the butt, a salesman, a newscarrier for the *Pittsburgh Post-Gazette*, and set the tone and pace for the rest of my life.

I wanted to introduce myself, and give you a little background, because I am going to be writing to you from this space from now on, and I want to get to know you better, too.

I've always loved sports. And I always loved to write about the games we played. When I was about 13, and in the eighth grade, I started writing stories about the games we were playing on Sunnyside Street and in nearby fields.

I organized a basketball league, and positioned spotlights in my parents' window that lit the area around the basketball hoop I erected across the street from our home. I also had a track and field team and passed out trophies to the youngest kids. And we played baseball and softball, and I cleaned up and raked neighborhood fields so we had a place to play. I kept statistics for everything we did. We had jerseys that proclaimed us as members of the Sunnyside A.C., and buttonholed local businessmen — beer distributors, shoe makers, shop keepers, numbers writers, you name it — to become boosters and help us buy our jerseys and equipment.

I learned to knock on doors and collect money when I was delivering the morning paper, and I was never afraid to do that.

I used my sister's typewriter, and some individual letter stamps I had purchased along with a small printing press at the Hazelwood Variety Store, and made up a one-page newspaper. I cut out pictures from national sports magazines and the local newspapers and changed the photo captions, putting the names of my friends under the photos. All-American players at Notre Dame, Pitt, West Virginia or Penn State became Butchie Boffo or Butchie Boyle, boyhood buddies of mine, or Snookie Pisan or Toby Lewis or Johnny Metro. I posted my one-page newspaper on the door of my home at 5410 Sunnyside Street.

It didn't cause as much of a stir as Martin Luther did when he posted his letter of protest on the door of the church of Wittenberg, but the kids in the neighborhood looked forward to finding their names and feats featured on our door.

One day I wrote a few paragraphs about a game between the Sunnyside A.C. and one from nearby Burgwin Field that featured a future pro football player named Dave "Rooster" Fleming and visited the local newspaper office and slipped my story under the door.

That week my three-paragraph story appeared in the sports page of *The Hazelwood Envoy*, a bi-weekly publication with a circulation of about 2,000. That was it; I was hooked.

I kept writing these short stories about the games on our street and slipping them under the door. And they kept printing them in the paper.

One day, when I was 14, I got a call from the owners of *The Hazelwood Envoy* and they wanted to see me. They had a sports editor's job opening and wanted to interview me. They didn't know I was so young and they were surprised to see how small I was. They named midget football after me. But they gave me a chance to write enough stories to fill two pages of their tabloid every other week — with my picture and my byline for $5 per issue — for the next five years.

That's when, as a sophomore at the University of Pittsburgh, I became the sports editor of *The Pitt News*. That's when I retired from *The Hazelwood Envoy*. I had a half scholarship, from Senator Robert Fleming of Aspinwall, when I went to Pitt, and picked up the other half at the start of my sophomore year when I became the sports editor of the student newspaper. It had always been a position held by seniors.

I was on the student yearbook and radio station staffs as well, and it was a terrific experience. During the summers of my college years, I had internships at *The Pittsburgh Press* and *The Philadelphia Evening Bulletin*.

From there, I've written for the U.S. Army Hometown News in Kansas City, a camp newspaper in Fort Greely, Alaska, during a two-year stint (1965-1966) when I was in the military service, and then Miami, New York and Pittsburgh. It was fun all along the way.

I bumped into a fellow from my hometown of Hazelwood while walking through the streets of downtown Pittsburgh midway through my pro writing career and he said, "I always envied you because you always knew what you wanted to do."

I had to smile because, after being involved in every possible area of sports and communications for over 30 years, I was still not sure what I really wanted to do. But I still loved sports and I still loved to write. And I love living where I live these days.

Every day, I see things or feel things that I would like to write about. Only now I see them in different neighborhoods of Pittsburgh. This is important to me. This is my home.

I thought about writing a story each week and posting it on the door of our home, but my wife, Kathie, wasn't too keen on the idea. She had a wreath there and wanted to keep it that way.

I could continue to write and edit national magazines, and I would soon start writing books about Pittsburgh sports achievement as well. I want to write about good people, about families and feelings, about movers and shakers, and adults and kids who merit attention. I feel that what is happening with my family reflects what others are experiencing with their own families. My stories are your stories, something you might be able to relate to because of your own family experiences .

I plan on being positive, and having some fun.

Jim O'Brien sits with Pal at rear of 5410 Sunnyside Street.

Bea Schwartz was
a special secretary

April 25, 1990

T his is the week when I would be out looking for an appropriate greeting card and gift for Secretary's Day. The card would have to be something different, a little daffy, something irreverent, maybe something saucy or spicy, a sexy blonde woman with a Mae West come-up-and-see-me-sometime look on her well-painted face.

Something like my secretary. She was the one who first suggested — in a stage whisper — that I should apply for the position of sports information director at the University of Pittsburgh when Dean Billick was promoted to assistant athletic director and there was an opening. Soon after, Billick contacted me and approached me about the job when I was a sportswriter at *The Pittsburgh Press*. Having Bea Schwartz as my secretary was the greatest perk of any job I have ever had.

My secretary hated birthday cards, and anybody who even hinted at her age, but she could live with Secretary's Day, though she always rebuffed any special attention. "Why the fuss?" she would ask. "What's the big deal? You didn't have to do this. You shouldn't have."

You could not take her to lunch or dinner. For her, life was a moveable feast. You snacked all day, when you felt like it. Give her candy and she would pass it out to the world. Anaclairs were her favorites. She was a chocoholic. Give her flowers and she would point them out to every passerby. And urge them to stop and smell the roses.

Bea Schwartz was some secretary. Bea Schwartz was something else. Bea Schwartz was special. She was my secretary for four years (1983-87). I used to tell her Bea was short for beautiful, or short for the best. "Get out of here," she'd say in a scold.

She was everybody's Auntie Mame. She was Aunt Bea to so many children, including a real niece named Mindy Keane who lived in Upper St. Clair. Bea would drive out to visit Mindy on special occasions, such as the Jewish holidays. Mindy has a sister named Cindy and Bea liked that. She liked rhymes.

Bea was my Jewish mother, in the best sense of the expression. Everybody should be so blessed. She cared about me and catered to me, as she did everybody in the sports information department at Pitt. She pushed you to be better, and praised you to the hilt. She promoted everybody she knew. Thoughtful was her middle name.

Her desk was a delicatessen. She'd spread cheese on a cracker and offer it for an eye-opener in the morning, along with freshly-brewed coffee. During Passover, she would give you coconut macaroons and matzos. She kept leftovers from our media luncheons and made the food last for a week. Sometimes two weeks, if you did not mind green edges on some hors d'oeuvres. The waitresses all loved her. "You can't believe how well she took care of us," one said.

She enriched everyone who passed her desk, with something she might say, with a smile, with a Pitt bumper sticker, the latest game program, a book, a balloon, an Anaclair, some kind of snack. "Can I get you something?" she'd ask. "What do you need?"

She handed out stuff to alumni, boosters and ballplayers, probably breaking a few NCAA rules along the way. She always had a supply of little toys to give to youngsters. Little cars and trucks.

She was the hostess for the media and Pitt staff at every sports event. She was always nicely dressed, usually with a bright bow ribbon in her bright blonde hair that matched her suit or dress. Like Rose Marie in the Dick Van Dyke Show. She was willing to dance with me around her desk when things got dull, and I would turn up the volume on the radio for a favorite slow song. It would put a smile on everyone's

Kathie and Jim O'Brien with his secretary Bea Schwartz

face in the office. Well, almost everyone. I think there was a woman on the staff who disapproved of our behavior. Or maybe she disapproved of dancing, I don't know.

Who else had a secretary who loved to shoot pool, who, indeed, carried her own stick, and screwed it together once you got to the pool table in the Faculty Club or the William Pitt Student Union?

She shot fast, and often one-handed and often beat you and some of Pitt's finest and most confident young athletes.

She could type with the best of them, knew how to spell better than anybody in the office, loved for you to test her with a tough word, was great at grammar, could write poems — though most of them were "R" rated — and was a star who stole the show at most office parties.

Bea Schwartz loved to bet on sports events, and wasn't happy unless she had something riding on most games. Even somebody else's games. She was always giving me $5 to give to my mother. "Give this to your mom for bingo," she would say, and would not take "no" for an answer.

When she inherited some money, she gave just about everybody in the office a share of it. She was always giving my daughters, Sarah and Rebecca, a handful of toys and candy and a few dollars or coins.

We were always rooting for her to hit the Lottery because we knew we would all be rich. Bea shared her money, and all her gifts. She was a giver. She was a throwback to another era, one of Damon Runyon's Broadway characters. She once worked for a radio station in McKeesport and was called "Hatbox Hattie" in a commercial she did.

She looked like a movie star from another day, and dressed the part. She'd had open-heart surgery, and was left with a large zipper-like scar from her Adam's apple down her chest, yet she always wore low-cut dresses and gowns for special evening occasions. From a distance, it gave her the appearance of great cleavage. She liked that.

She was a great storyteller. And no one laughed any harder at a good joke. Or a bad joke. WTAE's Bill Hillgrove left her in stitches every time he stopped by her desk to tell his latest joke. No one has more jokes to offer than "The Voice of the Panthers." She was a terrific audience.

When I saw her the last time at Presbyterian-University Hospital, she had balloons and banners and pictures of loved ones all over the room. At her bedside, she had a supply of books and bumper stickers and banners to give out to those who visited her. Just like another day at the office.

"Here's five dollars for your mother for bingo," she said in parting. "Give her my love."

Bea Schwartz died from cancer last month. She was 65. It was the first time I really knew her age. It really hurt. This is a preview, I thought, of what it will be like when my mother dies.

"Who's going to get all those wind-up toys she had on her desk?" asked my daughter Rebecca. I wondered what would happen to all the photos of the children of staff members that lined the edges of her desk.

The week after Bea died, I opened a fortune cookie at the Sesame Inn in Mt. Lebanon and found a saying that suited her well: "There is no wisdom greater than kindness." I slipped it alongside her photo in my wallet.

"It's a shame," said Art Rooney Jr. of Mt. Lebanon, vice-president of the Pittsburgh Steelers. "When I'd come to Pitt Stadium to scout the players, she'd really look after me. She always made me feel at home there. She'd sit next to me for awhile and talk. She enjoyed talking to everybody in the press box. In that sense, she was a lot like my dad."

Like Art Rooney, the founder of the Steelers, Bea Schwartz was a once-in-a-lifetime person.

"Familiar acts are beautiful through love."
— Percy Bysshe Shelley

Driving Miss Sarah a real trip

May 9, 1990

As of May 7, I will have two teenage daughters. I can wait. Sarah is 16 and will be 17 in September. Rebecca will soon be 13.

For the past two months, I have been teaching Sarah how to drive an automobile. Rebecca has been riding in the back seat on some of our sojourns through the South Hills, and taking it all in. I don't think I want to go over the same ground from the beginning when it's Rebecca's turn to take the wheel, so I let her go with us.

Sarah is doing just fine. She starts the car well, judges distances well, is starting to get more confident, and looks forward to our next outing. She's not afraid anymore. Rebecca is asking better questions. She's not afraid either.

My heart doesn't skip as many beats as it did in our initial forays, my stomach doesn't clutch as often, and I am learning to bite my tongue. Sarah doesn't need Solomon or Dick Vitale teaching her how to drive.

Rebecca keeps Sarah humble. No sooner does Rebecca settle into her seat and strap herself in, than she calls out, "Don't get us killed, Sarah! Don't go over any cliffs!" Sarah smiles, slips the car into its proper gear, most of the time anyhow, and we're off. "Sarah, I think I'll sue you for whiplash on that one!" cries Rebecca as we go bump into the afternoon.

Sarah still needs to get what I call road awareness, anticipating wrong moves by other drivers, sensing what will happen next, checking out the rear-view mirrors and speedometer regularly, seeing the whole picture, knowing the pitfalls that await you in certain places, looking back before changing lanes, respecting the awesome power of an automobile, relaxing a little. And she needs a lot of work on driving backwards and parking. But so do a lot of adults with drivers' licenses. One day one of her classmates was driving a car out of his garage and onto his driveway as we were coming down the main street. "What do I do?" Sarah asked.

"You just keep going, you have the right of way," I said, just before her friend pulled out right in front of us, and shot down the road past us. "Keep in mind," I said, "that there are other students out there like you who aren't sure what they're doing."

We practice parking at a park near our home, and I've noticed that all the animals she and Rebecca used to ride when we moved here 11 years ago have been painted for the spring and summer season. They look great and inviting. There are familiar faces on the duck, panda, turtle, dolphin and beaver. I remember teaching my girls how to ride them. It was easier teaching them how to ride a panda or a duck than driving an automobile. It seemed easier. Safer. But I was probably scared back then, too, worried that one of them would fall off and get hurt. Worrying goes with the title of father or dad.

For the first few weeks, I limited Sarah's driving to the streets around our home, mostly in and out of cul de sacs, safe stuff. She's taking driver's education at Upper St. Clair High School. The first day she went out with another classmate for driving time with her instructor at school. I asked her where they went. "He had us driving on Route 19," she said calmly.

"Route 19!" I said, not so calmly. "My God, why didn't he just have you drive at the Indianapolis Speedway for starters?"

Route 19 reminded me of teenagers who died there in auto accidents just a few years back, children of friends, and of other children of friends who are still recovering from being struck by an auto on that competitive stretch of highway. Damn, none of us wants that to happen to our children. We'd keep them in a cocoon if we could.

19

Not easy leaving Sarah at music camp at Chautauqua

July 18, 1990

Dear Sarah: How is life at Chautauqua? Hopefully, it's agreeing with you, and you are finding your way around, and making new friends and good music.

This is the first time you have ever gone to a summer camp, and you picked one that lasts seven weeks. You should be quite the cellist when you come back home after seven weeks of instruction, practice and recitals. I know you will handle it just fine. I hope I can handle it as well.

This should help prepare you for going off to college some day. I hope it prepares me for you going off to college some day. You are 16 now, and you just passed your driver's test before you went off to camp, and you're getting more mature and more independent.

I never went off to camp as a kid. I heard so many horror stories about the camp the kids in my neighborhood went to, about mattresses being hung out to dry after being wet on the night before, about bad food, etc., that I was never too enthusiastic about going. I think those were low-rent camps, not as classy as Chautauqua.

The first camp I ever went to was called Fort Knox, just outside of Louisville, Kentucky, and I didn't care much for it, not from the first day, even though I liked the food. Fort Knox is where our government stores its gold. It's also famous for training soldiers to operate tanks. I wanted to come right back home, but I had no choice since I had been drafted into the U.S. Army. It was stay at camp or stay in a prison. Some thought there wasn't much difference.

My second camp was in some forsaken outpost in Alaska. It was called Fort Greeley. It was the Army's Northern Warfare Training Center and Arctic Test Center. It was better than being in a camp in Vietnam. On reflection, I feel I am better off for all my military experiences. I'm glad I went.

It was difficult for Mom and me to say goodbye to you on Sunday. There were things I wanted to say to you, but I was tongue-tied as I hugged you. Imagine me not being able to express myself. I can't even put the right words down here, or say what's in my heart, because I want this to be a letter and not a novel.

Suffice to say, your mother and I are both excited for you about the opportunity this experience at Chautauqua provides. The place looks like a setting for Meredith Wilson's "The Music Man," and you will be surrounded for seven weeks by musicians, dancers and artists in an idyllic intellectual haven. You share a common language.

After we had said goodbye, I felt as if I hadn't said what I wanted to say, so I followed you down the hall. But the door to your room was already closed, and I heard you talking excitedly and enthusiastically to one of your new friends, and that made me feel good. It was time to go. You were on your own.

I felt bad as we drove away from Chautauqua. I think my heart is still somewhere amid all those pastel storybook cottages.

This will be a summer of personal growth for you, as a young person and as a musician. I believe you will come back more confident about yourself and your abilities.

During the registration, I was pleased to see how easily you fit in, and how the other kids were so friendly. You were smiling. When you are smiling, I feel good. I want my kids to be happy. Your sister, Rebecca, was at her grandparents' home for the weekend, so you know she was happy.

Grandpap and Grandma Churchman certainly love you guys.

While you were filling out forms, I was talking to Peter Leo, a columnist for the *Pittsburgh Post-Gazette*. His son, Steven, a sophomore at Taylor Allderdice High School, is there for the same music school. He plays the clarinet. He was there last year, too, and loved it. Steven said, "The kids here are real friendly, and I had a good time. That's why I'm back." That's encouraging.

I hope I beat Peter Leo to a column on the subject of summer camp, but maybe he did his last summer. He's a terrific writer. You can learn from other people who do something well in your field. So pay attention.

You will meet talented achievers from many different parts of the country. I met a young singer from San Antonio who is a San Antonio Spurs' fan, and we compared notes on the National Basketball Association. The young man goes to the Manhattan (N.Y.) School of Music, and you'll probably get to meet him. He might be impressed by your basketball knowledge.

The young girl who introduced herself to you right away is from Wisconsin, and I was aware of others from Boston and Brooklyn and Raleigh, North Carolina. Should be an interesting mix. I thought it looked like a casting call for "Fame" or for "Head of the Class."

Do you remember when we first pulled up to the stop sign outside Kellogg Hall, where you signed in, and two young women walked across the street in front of us? And I said, "If I were a young man coming here, I'd be saying, 'Hey, I'm going to like it here!'"

One of those girls was your roommate. Anastasia. Anybody named Anastasia has to be interesting. She's from Boston. There are lots of kids there from Boston, it seems. It will be interesting to hear how you say "Harvard" when you come home at the end of August. You might end up with a Boston accent.

Hope you have gotten what you need to make your room more comfortable (like another closet, huh?). But some of the parents told me they are nicer than most college dorms. Your room seems so small to me. Then again, I have this thing about needing space. And daylight. You adapt better.

You'll make out better than I would, I am sure. Your mother and I are proud of you, and we're going to miss you a great deal this summer. Your bedroom seems like a museum without you here. We'll be up to see you and we look forward to our visits and your letters. Take care, honey, and make the most of it. Love you. Dad.

Wearing her Chautauqua sweatshirt, Sarah blows out candles in celebration of her 17th birthday with her grandparents, Harvey, Mary and Barbara.

This Dreamland turns into a nightmare

October 24, 1990

Have you ever stayed at the Dreamland Motel? Bet you did, but under another name, or alias, something like the Nightmare Inn or Lost Honeymoon Hut, and signed the registrar as Mr. and Mrs. Jim Jones. Our family stayed at the Dreamland Motel in Deep Creek, Maryland, many moons ago, full moons mostly, but we will not soon forget the experience. For us, the Dreamland was a nightmare. There is no Dreamland anymore, only in our minds.

We were reminded of it twice in recent months. This summer, during one of our trips to Chautauqua, New York, to visit our daughter, Sarah, who spent seven weeks there at an orchestra camp, we couldn't get into the nearby Holiday Inn or Comfort Inn, where we had been most satisfied on earlier visits.

The only place we could get a room was a place called Journey's End. To us, that had an ominous sound. "Sounds like another Dreamland Motel," offered Rebecca, our younger daughter, who was traveling with us. We were unfamiliar with Journey's End, but it turned out be a very nice place, and is a very successful chain, with sites mostly in Canada.

Then Ted Frantz, a friend from Mt. Lebanon, sent us a real estate booklet from Deep Creek, loaded with classified listings. There, in full color — talk about gall — was the Dreamland Motel. It was for sale. Frantz had circled it with red ink.

"Thought you'd be interested," wrote Frantz, who must have had his tongue buried deep in his cheek.

The Dreamland is definitely a "handyman's special," and if you've been a faithful reader of this column you know that's not my bag of tools. If anybody should be interested in buying the place it ought to be Frantz. He and his wife own TEDCO Construction Co., Inc., a Carnegie-based company responsible for many new buildings around Pittsburgh. They were grooming their son, Jim, to take over the operation.

We stayed at the Dreamland Motel one memorable summer night, during a business stopover in Deep Creek, en route to a convention in Nashville, Tennessee. To get first-rate accommodations at Deep Creek during the summer, you have to book a room for a full weekend, or promise your second son to do their landscaping for at least two summers. We needed a room for just one night.

Wherever we called for a reservation, we were getting shut out, until we reached the Dreamland line. "The O'Brien family had visions of Marriotts, heated pools, room service and king-size beds on their minds," Sarah would later write in an essay at school. "But the family looked up and viewed the crummiest motel they had ever seen."

No sooner had we turned into the unpaved driveway of the Dreamland than Rebecca, who was about ten at the time, asked a loaded question: "Dad, why is there grass growing in the swimming pool?"

Sure enough, the plastic covering on the pool, which apparently hadn't been removed in several summers, had grass and plants growing on it. It was all mossy green. If that wasn't a tip-off to what awaited us, surely we should have known to drive on when we were greeted by the manager of the motel. He was a first cousin of Norman Bates, the motel keeper in Alfred Hitchcock's movie "Psycho."

Fortunately, the kids hadn't seen that movie at that stage of their lives. Now they laugh when they see it, not exactly what Hitchcock had in mind. To them, it's now in the same genre as the Chevy Chase "Vacation" movies. You can relate to that, right?

We were taken aback by our room. Half the room was painted orange, and the other half was painted white. Half the floor had carpeting, the other half tile. It looked like a creamsicle that had been left out in the sun too long.

There was a sink at the bottom of the beds, and the water in it had a sulfur odor and the basin had a rusty bottom. Really got you excited about brushing your teeth. There were ants on the floor of the bathroom, which I discovered when the bottom of my slacks smothered them. I pulled back the shower curtain carefully, expecting to find the long decayed corpse of Janet Leigh. Just more ants.

We had some time to kill — I wish I hadn't used that expression — before dinner, so we decided to lounge in the twin beds and watch some TV. The TV was set high on a shelf near the ceiling. My wife and I are both 5-8½, but she was the only one who could reach the dial on the TV, as her reach is about 2 inches longer than mine. It was a wasted effort.

We could get only one channel on the TV, and I think it was from Anchorage, Alaska. I had never seen so much snow since my Army days in the 50th state. So we took a nap on what turned out to be lumpy mattresses. You'd swear they were stuffed with stones from the unpaved driveway.

Dinner was outstanding, as the Frantz family hosted us at a nearby inn. But we were alarmed when we returned to the Dreamland and discovered that the door of our room was wide open. Kathie ordered me to enter the room first. We had left our bags and suitcases in the room, one containing her jewelry, and expected to find only orange and white, but none of our stuff. Nothing was missing. We had been spared. We counted our blessings.

It wasn't easy to get to sleep that night. The beds were so uncomfortable. Kathie ended up with bites all over her legs. This was a night when the bed bugs did bite. We did, however, fall asleep. In the middle of the night, the door sprang open with a frightening sound. The door hit the wall with a shotgun bang. I bolted up in bed, waiting for the worst. I fully expected "Texas Chain Saw Massacre II" to be reenacted right in our room at the Dreamland Motel.

Nothing happened. I checked the door and discovered that it was warped. That's why it kept coming open. It was badly warped. Like anybody who'd suggest you stay at the Dreamland Motel.

Sarah and Rebecca and their mother enjoy vacation trip.

"*Your living is determined not so much by what life brings to you as by the attitude you bring to life.*"
— **John Homer Miller**

Going back to Grove City

October 31, 1990

This was a weekend when Kathie O'Brien could be
Kathie Churchman once again. My wife had gone back
to Grove City College for a reunion of the Class of 1965
on the 25th anniversary of its graduation. She went there
with Sandy Allison, nee Sandy Rossi, who had been her
roommate all four years during their student days.

Kathie had come from McKeesport and Sandy from
Rochester, New York when they were first paired. They were
so different, they still are, and yet they got along fine and
remain friends.

Sandy had flown in from Florida two nights earlier. She
and Kathie had spent much of Thursday and Friday nights
browsing through their yearbook, the *Ouija*. Always the
ardent students, they were doing their homework for
Homecoming.

They wanted to be sure they knew who's who when
they got to Grove City. You can get to Grove City from the
South Hills in an hour and a half, but it's a trip back in time,
as are all reunions. It's an enlightening experience. Reunions
always make you consider where you've been, where you
are, and where you're going. It can be frightening to reflect
too much.

Among the things they discovered when they got there
was that the yearbook is now called *The Bridge. The Ouija* had
fallen into disfavor with the administration, something about
being associated with cults and Satanism. Oh well, so much
for tradition. Times change.

So do the names of yearbooks. Mine was called *The Owl*.
Now the Pitt yearbook is called *Panther Prints*. I don't know
what the owls did to fall into disfavor. Probably got old and
lost their feathers.

28

Kathie and Sandy — "the Sundance Kids" — noticed that some buildings that had been there when they were students had given way to parking lots, a lot of parking lots. When they were there, students were not permitted to have cars on campus. "Where can you go anyhow?" asked Sandy. "I'd rather they'd have kept the buildings. They used to have a gym with an oval track around the upper level, up in the rafters. You should preserve stuff like that."

They visited all the classrooms they once attended, and the dormitory rooms where they once resided. They remembered they had a poster of New York Giants star Frank Gifford on the back of the door. "Frank Gifford! Don't tell anyone that," Kathie warned. "That really dates us!"

Posters and pictures weren't permitted on the walls back then. They are now. "You couldn't see we had a poster when our door was open," said Sandy. They were daring, all right.

They visited the campus chapel, which they were required to visit about five to six times a week during their student days. It was mandatory. The requirements have since been reduced.

While at Grove City for the reunion, Kathie and Sandy went searching for a restroom, and were escorted into the women's locker room in the athletic facility. They had never been inside a locker room like that during their student days.

It was nice and clean, and so spacious. They wished they had brought towels so they could shower before changing clothes for an evening event. Touring a campus and attending reunion events can make you sweat.

There were more mirrors and bigger mirrors than they may have wanted. They fixed their makeup, and studied their reflections, and wondered how they looked, especially how they looked compared to when they were coeds on the campus. How had they held up? How did they look to the current students?

"Look at it this way," one of their former classmates suggested. "When we were juniors here, what would we have thought if we saw the Class of '39 walking around the campus at Homecoming?" There's a show-stopping question for you. The former classmate is not likely involved in counseling.

If they needed to be reminded, Kathie and Sandy both had been given nametags to wear at Homecoming, and they included copies of their yearbook photos, and their maiden and married names. So classmates could identify them.

Both were dark brunettes back then. Kathie still is, and without any help from her hair stylist, I like to boast. Sandy confused everyone. She had cut her hair shockingly short — she always liked to shock people — and dyed it blond. I thought they both were more beautiful than ever.

Sandy and Kathie have always been a contrast, but they have also been good for one another. They wish, of course, they could see more of one another. People always say that at reunions.

"The whole class of '65 has stopped smoking, except for me," said Sandy. "But I stopped drinking, and they didn't."

When Sandy said this to Kathie upon their return to our home, while window-shopping at the Galleria on a beautiful Sunday afternoon, Kathie said, "Sandy, you're outrageous. That's why I liked you. You always made me laugh. Jim's like that, too. That's why I married him."

Always the class clowns, Sandy and Jim, forever.

Former classmates came from as far as San Francisco and Bartlesville, Oklahoma, Kathie recognized only one from Pittsburgh, an attorney named Tommy Thompson. I always liked his name because the Philadelphia Eagles once had a quarterback named Tommy Thompson. He was with the Eagles at the same time they had another quarterback named Adrian Burk. Another beautiful name.

"A lot of attorneys come back," Kathie said. Tommy came with his wife, Judy, another Grover. He was the only fellow Kathie recalled, thank God.

Remember how I was worried about her going to this reunion because her relatives had met their second husbands at reunions?

Kathie and Sandy were among 91 from a class of about 400 students who had returned to Grove City for the silver anniversary reunion. That's pretty good. "That's a lot better than your class," said Kathie, reminding me of my own 25th anniversary reunion the year before that had disappointed me no end. But that's a story for another day.

Sandy couldn't stop talking about the reunion, about going back to Grove City. She hadn't been there since she graduated whereas Kathie had been back several times. Sandy didn't want to let go of Grove City. Or Kathie. Or our kids. They talked about how they seldom watched TV when they were at Grove City. They remembered seeing the Beatles when they made their first American appearance on the Ed Sullivan Show, the news about President Kennedy's assassination, and Sandy said she remembered watching Cassius Clay fight Sonny Liston. That was it.

Kathie O'Brien enjoys reunion with Grove City College roommate Sandy Allison.

Pining for the perfect Christmas tree

December 26, 1990

I have never had much luck with Christmas trees. They have always been too tall, too small, too fat, too thin, too dry, too vulnerable. Even when I think they're perfect. It all began back at 5410 Sunnyside Street in Glenwood with my Uncle Robbie. That's my earliest memory of a Christmas tree fiasco. I was about five or six at the time. My Uncle Robbie was in his early 40s and he was still a bachelor.

Uncle Robbie had been to a few bars before he came to our house. He was — as my dad, his older brother, always put it — half-crocked. He was with a date, a woman named Marie Blanche. It was the day before Christmas, which is my mother's birthday. My mother will be 84 this Christmas Eve. My Uncle Robbie died a few years back.

I was one of his pallbearers and, as I carried him to his grave, I remembered Uncle Robbie's Christmas Eve visit. He stumbled into our "front room" — no one ever called it a family room or living room — and he was obviously in no pain. Our Christmas tree was in the far corner of the room, about 15 feet from the door.

Uncle Robbie took an acrobatic dive — about a 2½ gainer without the benefit of a high platform — and plunged into our Christmas tree. He hit it like a heat-seeking missile. Our tree collapsed and Uncle Robbie fell face-first across the miniature railroad tracks that ran around the base of the Christmas tree. Unfortunately, Uncle Robbie did not fall on the deadly third rail. He knocked over the skaters on the rink that was really a little mirror.

Uncle Robbie recovered, but the tree didn't. By the following Christmas, he had gotten married — to a woman named Mary — and they bought a home in the neighboring community of Greenfield. Our family visited his home at Christmas time. He said we would all have to take off our shoes at the door before we could enter his home, something about a new carpet he didn't want soiled. My mother wanted to toss her snow boots into their Christmas tree as a gift exchange. She was furious.

That same year, my mother hung a three-foot decorated Christmas tree upside down from the living room chandelier to keep it out of harm's way.

A Christmas card came to us a few weeks back from Matt and Ruthie Swetonic, and their sons, Andrew and Nicholas, who live in New York. The card caused Kathie and me to smile, as it does each year.

We were living in New York when Matt married Ruthie. We went to a Christmas party at their midtown Manhattan apartment soon after. They warmed our hearts with a romantic tale of what it was like to buy their first Christmas tree together in a lot near the bright lights of Broadway.

They talked about a starry night, and sipping hot apple cider on the site, and kisses they exchanged, and how beautiful it had all been, as they brought their tree back to their first apartment in a light snowfall.

A few nights later, Kathie and I went to a nursery near our home on Long Island to buy our Christmas tree. We took our 15-month-old daughter, Sarah, with us. She was wearing her first snowsuit, a beautiful white one. "You only buy a white snowsuit for your first-born child," as Kathie says, "then you get smarter."

I remember the Korean couple that owned the nursery showed us trees. They were so friendly and in the spirit of the season. I held Sarah's hand most of the time, but she had been walking for about three months, and wanted to explore.

Suddenly, Sarah cried out. And then Kathie cried out. I turned to see that Sarah had taken a spill, right into a brown mud puddle amidst the Christmas trees. Her snowsuit was now half-white and half-brown. It was no longer beautiful. I didn't think this was what Matt and Ruthie had in mind.

For 23 years, we have always had a real Christmas tree, going back to our apartments in East Liberty, Miami and East Rockaway, New York. It has always been a struggle getting them set up.

For most of those years, once we had a house, I would find myself lying on the floor of the garage, working with a wrench or pliers, the way you would work under a car (which I have never done, by the way), to get the tree firmly bolted into the tree stand.

By accident a few years back, I discovered that you could do the same thing, and a lot easier, by turning the tree, instead of yourself, upside down. I knew how Edison felt when his first light bulb finally worked.

You are supposed to take a fresh cut off the bottom of the tree before you put it in the tree stand. One year, I cut off too much, maybe two inches too much. So I had to reattach the two-inch slice by pounding some nails into it. I felt like I was shoeing a horse.

I had always heard it was good for the tree if you put a few aspirin into the water. But I was always out of aspirin by the time I was finished assembling the tree.

After we had decorated the tree this year, I plugged in the lights, and heard a disturbing sound. I told Kathie about it. I said I thought something might be wrong with the plug. While I was out of the house, Kathie plugged in the Christmas tree lights. The plug went KAPOW!!! Kathie told me it sparked, sizzled and blew up in her hand. She was left with a black palm, but, thankfully, was lucky not to have been burned.

I came home and had to remove the bottom string of lights on the Christmas tree without disturbing the decorations. It looks all right without the string of lights. But the kids weren't crazy about this year's tree. Now that they are older, Sarah and her sister, Rebecca, are more critical of the tree each year. They never like the tree we pick.

We had been buying our trees at a nursery in Scott Township, but switched this time because we got a dry, brittle tree last year, and the needles fell off every time anyone touched the tree. This time we went to a nursery in Bethel Park. This year's tree is short and stout, and full, maybe too full. A friend said it reminded him of a "jolly, fat friar." That's when I figured the kids may be right, even if too honest for their own good.

Next year Kathie and I are going to let the girls go out and buy our Christmas tree. We're going to suggest they wear their white winter coats. And maybe their mother, with her blackened hand, can pat them on the back and wish them good luck as they leave the house.

Rebecca and Sarah play in the snow at their new home in Pittsburgh in 1979.

Saying goodbye to your mother is difficult

May 15, 1991

No sooner do I say hello to my mother these days than I start thinking about how I am going to say goodbye. What if it's the last time I say goodbye? So, more and more, I tell her why she has been so special in my life.

My mother is 83 and she will be 84 this Christmas Eve. She wasn't feeling well and she was in discomfort for two weeks last month, and there was some discussion about surgery. I was worried. But that was dismissed, mostly because of her age. She has been taking some medication, and she has bounced back. Right now, she is in relatively good health. She has always bounced back.

Mary O'Brien is a tough customer. She bounced back from a broken hip — she fell coming out of church, which didn't seem right — about four years ago and was able to walk without assistance within a year after the accident. She suffered a broken shoulder a year later, but healed quickly, and also recovered from several strokes.

She bounced back from a near-fatal pancreatic attack about six years ago. One night, during a three-month stay at Mercy Hospital, she thought she was dying. Everyone in the family was at her bedside except me. I was in DuBois speaking to high school students at a sports award banquet. I was in touch with her doctor over the telephone. He had told me it would be all right for me to go.

My mother said she felt herself going down a long tunnel, which had a blazing white light throughout, and she thought she was going to heaven. But she said, "Jimmy's not here; I can't go now."

Thank God I was in DuBois that night. I was pinch-hitting for Pittsburgh sports broadcaster Bill Hillgrove, and I have often thanked him for asking me to appear in his stead.

One of these days, I realize my mother is going to take a trip down that long white tunnel and never return.

We celebrated Mother's Day at our home recently with my mother and my in-laws all present. Mother's Day always reminds us to take time out and say "thank you" and to tell our mothers how we feel about them, and what they mean to us. Or it reminds us of how much we miss our mothers.

My dad died in 1968 at the age of 63. He was a good guy, but difficult for my mother. Yet she always speaks of him in a positive manner. She is a positive person. She still loves him. She still misses him.

She is always cheerful. She has had more than her share of tragedies, but has always come back strong. She still has a gleam in her eyes, even if she has to put drops in them to clear up one condition or another. She never complains. She takes her pills to keep her blood pressure down, and to keep everything else running smoothly. She has no heart problems, no cancer. We have been lucky.

There is a Jewish proverb that says God couldn't be everywhere and therefore he made mothers. President John Quincy Adams once said, "All that I am my mother made me."

Steelers' coach Chuck Noll says, "The people who deserve more recognition are mothers and housewives. They should be honored more often."

I agree with all of those observations.

My mother has always been there for me. I think she would do anything to help me. She is still a good speller and knows her grammar well. It wasn't that long ago that she joined my wife Kathie in proofreading my magazines and books for me. She would sell them on street corners for me if I asked her. And I just might.

She always believed me even when she shouldn't have. She let me make major decisions, even when I might have been too young or too impetuous to be left to do that.

My mother worked a swing shift when I was in grade school, working early some days, and late the next day. So I would have lunch at home one day, and lunch at one of the restaurants or drug stores near where she worked on the next day. I thought it was an adventure to eat at Isaly's when I was a youngster.

We still enjoy having lunch together. I see her about three times a week, and we talk on the telephone about three times a week. She has a young voice. I bring her only good news. I still want to please her and impress her. I never wanted to disappoint her. She knows me better than most. When I tell how busy I am, she still says, "Good, it will keep you out of trouble." Others might doze off during my intrepid tales, but my mother can't get enough. She always listens. Who will I call when she is gone?

When I say goodbye these days, I hug her longer and longer. She has gotten so small. I feel so tall. Like our roles have been reversed. I think she likes it that way. I know she likes those long hugs by the smile on her face. I have always been told how much I look like my mother. So someday that face will be mine. As long as she is alive, I will be somebody's child. I can still think of myself as a kid. I like it that way. So I don't want to say goodbye.

Bailey visits Mary O'Brien at Asbury Heights, an assisted-care residence in Mt. Lebanon.

Snake dance becoming
a family tradition

September 4, 1991

I figured my family was ready for school to start. They had all been in the sun too long. This has been one of the hottest, driest summers on record, and it had obviously taken its toll on more than our grass.

I was returning home from Borders Book Store on a sunny afternoon, having heard Bob Firth discuss his new book, *Pittsburgh Figured Out*, when I found my family in strange costumes in our driveway. Now I needed a book to figure out my family. Who doesn't?

They were dressed and behaving strangely. Perhaps I caught them by surprise. Rebecca, who is now a freshman in high school, was wearing white winter boots, a scarf around her neck, and draped over her head was one of the towels I use to dry off my car when I wash it.

She was wielding a shovel in a strange manner, a shovel that had not been touched since the last time it snowed. She appeared to be digging up the last patch of green grass that remains in our front yard.

Her sister, Sarah, a senior in high school this year, was jumping up and down nearby. She wasn't wearing boots, but she, too, had a scarf around her neck, and was wearing a blue and gold Pitt tassel cap. Keep in mind it was moving toward 90 degrees on the thermometer that day. Their mother, who was eager for school to start again, was also wearing a scarf around her neck, and a tam on her head. "There was a snake in the garage when we got home," Kathie shrieked. For the record, Kathie is a calm sort who seldom shrieks.

"Rebecca told us this is what we should wear to go after a snake," said Sarah. "So it wouldn't bite us or poison us."

I got out of the car, with some trepidation, I must admit, and carefully came up behind Rebecca. She was having a good time, like her sister and mother, with this bit of Sunday madness.

"Dad, don't write a column about this," Rebecca blurted out before I could come to her rescue, or at least her side. Squiggling on the blade of her shovel was a six-to-seven-inch garter snake, identifiable by its longitudinal stripes. In tales later told about this episode, the snake would grow in size, to where it was at least a foot long, and as fat as a sausage. Rebecca dropped it a safe distance from our front door.

Kathie said its tongue was this long, and it kept darting in and out. Scary stuff. At least, no one suggested it was a python or boa constrictor. Because of the long, hot summer we have had more than our share of bees and wasps hanging around our house. And now we were being invaded by snakes. Our next-door neighbors had a similar snake-in-the-garage story to share, only they hadn't dressed up for the event. I was only two days away from my 49th birthday and, in my mind anyhow, my 50th birthday as well. I was motoring too fast toward that 50th birthday, and needed to slow down. I needed to be reminded of my youth, and more carefree days. My family did that for me with their impromptu snake dance. When I was about 13 or 14, about the same age as Rebecca, I used to enjoy spending an occasional day hiking through Sugar Hill, a woodsy area about a half-mile from my home in Glenwood, just above the Glenwood Bridge that crosses the Monongahela River and connects the community with Hays and West Homestead.

I would take along a younger traveling companion, a scout, a fearless kid named Joey Buffo. He was my sidekick. Every cowboy on TV — The Lone Ranger, Hopalong Cassidy, The Cisco Kid — had a sidekick back then. I wanted one, too. We would search the hillside for animal life, and turn over stones in the streams to find crayfish and salamanders. And, sometimes, we'd find snakes. Joey Buffo would pick them up with his bare hands. One day, we brought two of those snakes back to my home.

Joey put them in a box, and put a screen over the box so the snakes could breathe. And we went upstairs to watch some cowboy movie on TV. The next thing I knew I heard my mother scream. She had just come home from work, and this was not the usual way she let me know she was home.

I raced downstairs to see what was wrong, but had an idea that my snakes were somehow involved. I found my mother standing on a chair, and two snakes slithering around on the floor in front of our refrigerator.

"Don't you ever bring home snakes again!" my mother reprimanded. And I never did.

Seeing my family dancing around in the driveway that Sunday made me smile, and so did the memory of my mother standing on that chair in our kitchen.

Sarah, Kathie, Jim and Rebecca

Why do daughters grow up so quickly?

October 16, 1991

I saw the daughter of one of our neighbors in their driveway the other day. She and her mother were cleaning her car. I had not seen her in several months — she is married now and lives in Ohio — and I should have stopped to say hello. Sarah Shortridge and her mother Margo Shortridge and the rest of their family have always been favorites of mine.

I should have honked the horn, anyway, as I passed, but I was in a big hurry, and had no time to talk. And it will be months before her parents or I will see her again.

Two other daughters of two other neighbors came to mind. One is in Orlando these days, the other lives in LA, and we see them so seldom, usually for a wedding or a funeral. I was also worried about the well-being of another neighbor's daughter.

All four of those daughters used to be baby-sitters for my two daughters. Now they're all in their mid-20s, and they will be having their own daughters and sons soon enough.

Now my two daughters do the baby-sitting in our neighborhood, and soon my Sarah won't be doing that, either, and Rebecca will be the only baby-sitter in our house. In September, Sarah celebrated her 18th birthday. I'm not sure I did. Somehow 18 seems too much older than 17, and sweet 16 seems just like a sweet memory.

"Do you realize," my wife Kathie commented to me that same night, "that this could be the last time Sarah celebrates a birthday in our house?"

When I mentioned that comment to my mother when we had lunch together the next day, she offered, "Do you realize she can get married without your consent?" And mothers are supposed to comfort us.

Sarah did seem to be walking with a swagger — not quite as bad as Barry Bonds, but close — looking a little more independent, now that she's of legal age. "Do you realize I can vote now?" said Sarah.

She is a senior in high school now, and her sister is a freshman. They had open house at the high school recently, and Kathie and I attended the sessions with Sarah's teachers, and I with Rebecca's teachers. Some of the latter used to be Sarah's teachers, and it seems like only yesterday that I was seeing those teachers at another open house.

In recent years, I always loved watching two television shows with the girls, namely "Doogie Howser, M.D." — about a child prodigy doctor — and "Wonder Years" — about a young boy who is always thinking aloud, mostly about girls.

But now Doogie is 18, and Kevin Arnold, as played by Fred Savage in "Wonder Years" isn't far behind, and both started off this season in a sweat over girls. Suddenly, these shows are as steamy as some of the daytime soap operas. I thought even the promos for these season-openers should have been X-rated.

Kathie baked a cake for Sarah's birthday, but Sarah was in such a hurry that night — she has had such a busy schedule — that we had to sing "Happy Birthday" to her before the rest of us sat down to dinner. Then she was off to some school activity.

Sarah sat at the head of the table with a single slice of cake on a plate in front of her, with a single candle stuck in the middle of that single slice of cake. Somehow, it didn't seem right. It wasn't enough to mark the occasion.

I wanted more candles and more people. One of Sarah's friends held a surprise party for her the next night, and I was happy to hear about that. A real party. A single candle for Sarah simply wasn't enough.

She is sending in applications for college now. She and Rebecca are both wearing sweatshirts with the names of colleges across the chest. It's exciting stuff.

Sarah wants to go away to school, but she says she doesn't want to go that far away. So why do Tulane and Stanford keep sending her stuff? Those schools are in New Orleans and northern California. A woman who reads this column told me on the telephone recently that she had just taken her daughter off to college, to Indiana University of Pennsylvania, which isn't that far away.

"I cried all the way home," she reported. "Then I thought about my dad because I used to call him whenever I wasn't feeling so hot, and he'd make me feel better. But he died this past year, so I started crying all over again about that." If it's not one thing, then it's another.

"Did Sarah come home yet?" Kathie asked me as I slipped into bed just before midnight on a recent Saturday night. "Yes," I said. "Why do you think I'm coming to bed? Now I can sleep."

Sarah and Rebecca make faces at their father.

Sled riding is good for the heart

February 5, 1992

I wonder if I will ever go sled riding again. In my travels through the South Hills this winter, I have watched with envy as parents and their children were sled riding. I saw them sailing down hillsides in the parks in Dormont, Mt. Lebanon and Bethel Park and, closer to home, on the hill that runs from the edge of the golf course at the St. Clair Country Club down to McLaughlin Run Road.

I have noticed that the sleds and coasters are a lot more colorful this winter, with green, yellow, blue and pink ones providing quite a contrast to the white backdrop. And a lot of them don't look much like sleds.

One day, as I was driving along McLaughlin Run Road with my two teenage daughters in the car, and observing the sled-riding activity, I asked them — somewhat in jest — if they wanted to take one last ride on those hills. They gave me that are-you-crazy? look I have become increasingly familiar with now that they are young adults.

I miss them being children. I miss the way they looked up at snowy hills when we were pulling along our sleds. I miss the way they looked up at me. Like I was the great wise guide who knew the way.

Mark Malone, the former Steelers quarterback, was telling me how much he enjoyed taking his 14-month-old twins, a boy and a girl, for their first sled rides. "I loved it," he said. "So did they. They didn't want to go home."

I miss tumbling off the sled with the girls falling off my back. We'd end up in a heap in the snow. I miss the wind in our faces, the snow in our mouths, the snow on our eyelashes, even the snow in our ears. I miss the laughing over our spills, the shrieks when you hit the bad bumps, or just missed hitting someone with your sled.

Sarah and Rebecca have fun on their sled in early days in Pittsburgh.

Lynn Cullen was talking about sled riding on her talk show on WTAE Radio the other day. A man called in and mentioned that he had a Flexible Flyer in his youth. That's what we had, too. I remember waxing the red runners so the sled would sail faster. There had been a rash of sled-riding accidents locally, and Cullen was suggesting that maybe youngsters should wear helmets like they do when they ride bikes. She mentioned how dangerous it really was.

The man told how he and his pals used to play a game on sleds that "was like Ben Hur in the chariot races."

It struck a familiar note. We called the game "Carry the Mail." You rode two to a sled. One of us would lie flat on the sled and steer it, spreading our legs wide so our buddy could kneel in the back of the sled. He rode shotgun and his job was to fend off assailants.

The team that was carrying the mail would get a two-step lead on the rest of the pack and the others would pursue the "mail-carrier" down the hill on the street where we lived, and try to knock you off your sled, or run you off the road. Along the curbs, there were sewers that could swallow the sled if not the passengers. I recall how your gloved hands would get scraped along the curb from time to time. There were other sledding paths on nearby hills and roads, and the more treacherous they were the more appeal they seemed to have for us. There were steep drainage ditches alongside some of them, and my pals were prone to try to push anyone carrying the mail into them, the deeper the better.

There were brick walls and fences and stone stairways and pipes on these obstacle courses. It's a wonder any of us survived those sled rides. It was especially good fun, and even more precarious, to do this in the dark of the night.

It's funny how reckless we are as kids, and how cautious we become as adults. We were fearless, yet we fear so much for our kids, whether they are riding sleds or riding in cars. Is it fair?

I will never forget the day we were sled riding at a recreation camp in upstate New York when Sarah was about five years old, and Rebecca was almost two. We were at a church-sponsored family weekend retreat.

There was a very steep incline where the sledding activity was going on. The hill ran about two hundred yards on a 45-degree angle toward a well-frozen lake. You finished the sled ride by sliding out on the ice.

Some teenage girls approached us at one point and asked if they could take Sarah with them on a toboggan. They seated Sarah in the front of the toboggan, right behind the curved front edge, and three of them sat behind her. As I surveyed the scene below I noted that there was only one obstacle on the sled run. There was a single tree at the bottom, just above the lake. I cautioned the girls to steer clear of the tree.

No sooner had they started down the hill, however, than I had this chilling fear that they were heading straight for that tree. Don't ask me how I knew that.

Now that hill was steep and slick, the snow packed hard, like a ski run. And I started running down the hill. I was hollering at them to turn the toboggan in a different direction. I couldn't have kept my balance under normal circumstances on that hill if I had been wearing mountain-climbing boots. It's strange what we can do in a crisis.

Like a heat-seeking missile, those kids were on target to hit that tree.

They veered at the last moment, and I swear I saw Sarah's head strike the tree. I thought she hit it flush and as hard as possible. My heart sank. It looked so bad.

When I reached the kids, they were all spilled out of their sled. And they were laughing. Sarah said she was fine. She smiled at me.

"What's wrong. Dad?" she said. "You don't look so good."

Wary of a fast break
in West Virginia

March 18, 1992

I was motoring through the mountains of West Virginia, wary of anybody I saw by the roadside. Before I left Pittsburgh a few days earlier, my mother had called and warned me not to stop and pick up any hitchhikers. Two of the three murderers who had escaped from the Moundsville Prison were still on the loose.

"I know I sound like a mother," she said in a strong, vibrant voice that belies her 85 years, "but you be careful. Don't stop for any strangers."

I smiled. My mother will always be my mother, and she will always be praying that I come home safely. I remember when I used to travel with sports teams around the country and how my mother always knew what awaited me where I was going.

If I were traveling west with the Steelers to Denver, she would tell me there was a snow storm coming out of Pike's Peak, and that I should take a scarf or snowboots. I am just as bad with my two daughters. "Be careful," I will say as they leave the house to walk around the block to go baby-sitting. "Watch yourself."

It was dark and the highway was a winding road, with occasional curves that made you lean into them, and I was grateful it wasn't snowing or raining. Then it really would have been a test of my driving skills. My daughter Sarah was asleep in the back seat of our car and I was up front by myself, eager to get us home safely. We had been on the go for about 12 hours, and we had about four more hours of driving ahead of us.

We had just come out of Beckley where we had stopped to get a late dinner and to get some gas. Twice on this trip I had been running too long on empty. Why? I had passed nine service stations where the unleaded regular was 99.9 cents per gallon, and I wanted to find one that was selling it for 96.9 or 97.9. Instead, I ended up having to go to a station that was selling it for 111.9. At least twice I feared that I would run out of gas halfway up one of those mountains. Imagine that predicament. I coasted down several of them with the car in neutral, like I did when I was a teenager, to save some gas.

I had seen a sign for the local daily, *The Beckley Gazette*, and recalled that I had a sergeant in the U.S. Army named Flip Morin who had been a sportswriter for that newspaper. Sgt. Morin was my immediate boss when I was the editor of a camp newspaper called *The Buffalo* when I was stationed in Fort Greely, Alaska.

I remember hitchhiking about a thousand-mile stretch across Alaska once in the company of a fellow soldier, a black man named Harold Johnson. We got picked up by an old grizzled gold miner whose jeep would shake if he went over 40 miles per hour, and later we were picked up by a lead-footed woman who obviously knew no fear.

Once upon a time, I used to hitchhike and I used to pick up hitchhikers. I had long since quit doing either. I still bump into a fellow who was the last man I picked up back in 1980 or 1981. His buddies had left him behind when they were checking out the Steelers at St. Vincent College. They were in two cars and they figured he was in the other car. I picked him up on Route 30 near the Mountain View Inn in Greensburg and brought him to Pittsburgh. He remains grateful to this day.

I saw about four hitchhikers on the way down through West Virginia, and about as many coming back up. It takes about four hours to drive the length of West Virginia, so we saw one about every hour.

Some were so dirty they looked like they had just come out of a coal mine. Or a tunnel under the Moundsville Prison. My mind was playing tricks on me, thanks to my mother. Who in their right mind would pick up those people? How would they ever get wherever they were going? Yet I did see a car stop and pick up one of the hitchhikers.

In Beckley, I also stopped at the local drug store to get some cough medicine for Sarah, who was fighting a cold. The pharmacist was watching the West Virginia-Duquesne basketball game on a TV set that sat on the floor behind the counter.

"Who are you rooting for?" I asked, just to tease him.

"I'm rooting for West Virginia." he replied.

"I'd have to root for Duquesne," I said.

"Yeah, I notice you're a Pitt man," he said, pointing toward a monogram on my blue sweater. "You root for those Pittsburgh teams."

That's another reason I am always nervous enough when I am in West Virginia. There were Pitt decals on the windows of both sides of my car. I don't need to see a sign that reads "Caution — Falling Rocks" to wonder if a rock might come flying through one of my windows.

Seeing the TV in the drug store prompted me to put a search on my radio for a station on the Mountaineer Sports Network. I picked up a station in Charleston and heard the familiar voice of a friend, Jack Fleming of Mt. Lebanon, who has been doing West Virginia basketball for about 40 years. In his prime, Fleming was the finest basketball broadcaster in the country. Hearing him and Woody O'Hara had a comforting effect on me.

I really enjoyed listening to the broadcast. They were good company and helped keep me alert. It reminded me of my youth and listening in the darkness of my bedroom to Joe Tucker describing the Duquesne basketball games. I loved the Dukes of Dick Ricketts, Si Green and Jim Tucker, and wanted to go to school there to study journalism. But I got a scholarship to Pitt and that was it. Thankfully, that worked out just fine. Sarah and I had been on a four-day tour of colleges in North Carolina and Virginia, as she searches for the right school for her. Her world is much broader than mine was. Pitt and Duquesne are too close to home.

It seemed perfect to be listening to a West Virginia basketball game going through those mountains. Just like it's special to sit on a porch at night, with no distractions, and listen to Lanny Frattare and Steve Blass doing a Pirates' radio broadcast. Somehow in the dark, you can see the game better. You have to use your imagination.

When I came back to my car I noticed that I had forgotten to lock the doors. Sarah was still sleeping in the backseat. Her window was cracked just enough to let some air in. I was upset with myself for failing to lock the doors while I was in the store. Thinking about what might have happened to her if those escaped prisoners had passed by was upsetting. How could I have been so careless? I like to beat myself up over such oversights.

P.S. Two days after we were in Beckley, police caught one of the escapees there.

Rebecca and Sarah

Getting out of line
in a funeral procession

April 1, 1992

Funerals remind us of other funerals. So it follows that funeral processions remind us of other funeral processions. Like the sadness and tears that accompany both, they tend to back up on us.

I saw two funeral processions in the past month, both on Rt. 19, that reminded me of earlier funeral processions, one from my youth and the other from the start of this year. The other day I was driving to downtown Pittsburgh, and spotted a funeral procession coming the other way in Banksville. I noticed that one of the cars in the middle of the procession had blown a tire. Talk about double trouble.

It brought to mind a funeral procession for one of my grandparents back in the mid-50s. We were headed to East Brady, Pennsylvania, about 50 miles northeast of Pittsburgh along the Allegheny River.

It was a tortuous demanding trip in those days, with lot of hills and narrow winding roads. In my family, we go a long way to bury our dead. In my family, the burials have always been in East Brady or Wheeling, West Virginia. In my mind, that is their legacy.

I was in the backseat of a car driven by my Uncle Phil. We used to call him "Short-Cut" Phil because he was always taking short cuts, and usually getting lost. He was a sober sort. Uncle Phil had the perfect face for a funeral.

My brother and I were egging him on, urging him to go faster, to take a short cut, as we traveled in the middle of a funeral procession. Uncle Phil's fuse was growing short. So was the rubber on his tires. We started smelling burnt rubber and the next thing you knew a tire blew out, with a bang. Uncle Phil held the road, fixed the flat, and we rejoined the procession at the cemetery.

That's all I remember about that funeral. But it set a precedent for getting out of line on the way to the cemetery.

Funerals are serious stuff. Maybe my family is irreverent, or just Irish, but every funeral is an Irish wake with us. We tend to laugh as well at most of our funerals. It is one extreme or the other. I think you need to do both to survive such setbacks.

I remember at my father's funeral, for example, when we first saw him laid out in the casket, my mother noted that his hair wasn't as dark or slicked down as it usually was. My dad used a lot of Vaseline to darken his hair. "Oh, your dad would die if he saw his hair like that," my mother remarked. She was serious. We all laughed.

Last month I was driving south on Rt. 19 from Upper St. Clair to McMurray, taking my lawn mower for its annual checkup to the Sears Service Center opposite The Gallery. I came upon a long funeral procession that was in the left lane for some reason. I later spotted them in front of the chapel at the Forest Lawn Cemetery. They were in the left lane — mighty early — to make a left turn.

I was in the right lane, and needed to make a left turn, but couldn't get over into the left lane because half the procession was still trailing me and proceeding to Sears, but I squelched that urge. I had already cut into one too many funeral processions for this year. Enough was enough.

Back in January, I was driving the third car in a long funeral procession departing a church in Hays. The funeral director had poor directions, as far as I was concerned, and took a route that cost us at least a half-hour at the start. Plus the procession was headed for Wheeling, which is 60 miles away, and much too far to travel in a procession. We went through Baldwin, Whitehall, South Park and into Upper St. Clair. We were traveling at about 25 to 30 miles an hour in a herky-jerky manner that was turning my stomach into turmoil. I could not handle this routine all the way to Wheeling; I'm sorry.

When we hit McLaughlin Road in my neighborhood and were about to make a left turn up onto Rt. 19, I told my fellow travelers I was cutting out of the funeral procession. This was another parade where I was out of step, just like in my Army days.

I was traveling with my wife, Kathie, and my mother and sister. They wondered what I was doing. We were five minutes from our house, and I said we were going home for a break.

Everybody in our car went to the bathroom, and we all grabbed a donut or made a sandwich, picked up a coffee or soft drink, and refreshed ourselves. It took about 20 minutes. We all felt better.

I told them we would catch up to the funeral procession. They didn't believe it could be done. Kathie wanted me to take the funeral home's flag off the hood of my car, but I insisted it stay. "I don't believe this," said my mother. "But I should be used to it by now."

Somewhere, just before the West Virginia border, I spotted a funeral procession ahead, moving along at about 40 miles per hour in the right lane. I smiled.

"OK, just fall in behind them," my wife advised.

"No," I said. "I'm going to get back into our old spot. We had the No. 3 position."

"I don't believe this," my mother said. "Oh, Jim, you're just too much."

So we zoomed along in the left lane. Family and friends who happened to look to the left from the funeral procession saw us streaming by, our flag fluttering in the wind. They must have thought they were in a Benny Hill movie.

I put on my turn signal, waited for an opening, and moved back into my spot in the procession. It was like we were never gone.

June was just busting out all over

July 1, 1992

I will be hard-pressed to match the month of June for sheer excitement and events that were both significant and satisfying. I hope July and August are equal to the challenge. For a sports fan, there was much to draw upon. The Penguins delivered a second straight Stanley Cup championship. The Pirates pulled out front, following some difficult days on the West Coast, and gave promise of a third straight NL East title.

The Chicago Bulls beat the Portland Trail Blazers for a second straight NBA title, and there was the French Open for tennis fans and the U.S. Open for golf fans. And I had a chance to spend a day at the Oakmont Country Club — one of America's sports shrines — with friends and some of the greatest players of all time.

For a father, or any parent, June is always a wonderful month. But this year was particularly special at our house. Our oldest daughter, Sarah, graduated from Upper St. Clair High School. She was one of 15 valedictorians in her class. Three of her long-time friends — Kara Pociask, Jenny Jackson and Michelle Roos — were similarly honored. They pushed each other to excellence.

There were other students who had distinguished themselves, such as Kavita Babu, Lee Ann Kelly and Hollee Schwartz, who I remembered had caught my attention as early as kindergarten or in grade school because of their precociousness and charm.

Our younger daughter, Rebecca, completed her freshman year at the high school with high honors. She said it was her most enjoyable school year yet. She had a good time.

So there was the end-of-school joy, a prom, plenty of graduation parties, the school picnic at Kennywood Park. I didn't get to go to Kennywood with the kids, and I felt left out. I drove Rebecca and four of her friends to the entrance of Kennywood and that was as close as I came to the amusement park and its world-famous roller coasters.

Rebecca and her best friend, Amber Kraus, were in the same numbers for the annual recital of the Janet Hays Dance Studio. There were 42 dance numbers in all, I think, challenging the loyalty and love of the family members in the audience.

There were family reunions and there was Father's Day. I would like to have spread so many good times over a longer period. I slept well in June. It was a month of emotions. There were too many times when it was difficult to make up one's mind whether to smile or shed a tear.

I was stunned when I saw Sarah in her prom gown the first time. "How do I look, Dad?" she asked. I didn't answer right away. "Very mature," I managed to say. I was reminded of how much more grown up my prom date looked when I called on her way back when. Or how Sarah's mother looked when I saw her the first time in her wedding gown.

I knew Sarah was in for a special evening when her prom date, a gifted musician named Patrick Werner, showed up at our house in a beautifully restored cream-colored 1940 Packard convertible driven by its owner, Ed Coyne. It was different from all the stretch limousines the kids believe are their birthright for such special outings these days. She was going out in grand style.

They were going, with 16 other friends, to dinner at LeMont on Grandview Avenue on Mt. Washington. Their prom was at The St. Clair Country Club. The post-prom party was at Faces in the Great Southern Shopping Center in Bridgeville.

I slept well that night, too, but I also woke up the instant Mr. Werner drove his own car into our driveway at about 5:30 a.m. following the post-prom lock-up party. Then I fell back to sleep.

It was a month that pushed a parent's emotions to the limit. I was pleased that my mother and my wife's mother and father — all proud grandparents — were there to share our joy. I enjoyed the smiles I saw on the faces of friends.

There were flowers and cards and freshly printed yearbooks and cakes and cookies and all kinds of wonderful food offerings, and happy people wherever we traveled. We spent more time with our neighbors then we had in a long time.

These events, we also learned, were sad for some, for one reason or another. We all get challenged some way. Some people's joys are other people's disappointments. Another school year is over and the swimming pools and recreation parks are open for the summer. There will be more outings and picnics and vacations and getaway weekends.

In her valedictorian speech, Jenny Jackson said something about "my childhood from which I shall soon be separated." That thought has stayed with me. I'm not sure I'm ready for that.

I was flipping through our family photographs, trying to find the right ones for a display at Sarah's graduation party. I enjoyed being reminded of so many people and places in our lives.

I noted the remarkable changes that have occurred through the years with our daughters and their friends, and our family and friends. I saw pictures of too many people who are no longer with us, and would be missing our celebration. How much time has passed so quickly?

As I walked to my car following the graduation ceremonies, I saw a father and his daughter just ahead of me. They were walking to their car as well. I walked behind them for about 200 yards. She was about four or five years old. She wore a white blouse and pink shorts. Her socks were white and turned down about two inches at the top, and had pink fringe. She wore a big pink ribbon in her brown hair. She had dimples all around her knees, like those Cabbage Patch Kid dolls.

I wanted to say something to her father. But I didn't. I wanted to tell him that he would be there, for her own high school graduation, before he knows it.

Sarah and Rebecca pose on front steps of Upper St. Clair home.

Cruising Pittsburgh's rivers and reminiscing

July 29, 1992

T he neon lights from the Alcoa billboard, all blues and violets, reflected on the waters of the three rivers and the spray from the fountain at The Point. They mixed with the bright lights of Grandview Avenue. There was a full moon. And the view from the upper deck of the Majestic, one of the many sternwheelers in the Gateway Clipper fleet at Station Square, couldn't have been better. I have seen it before, but it always makes me feel good about being a Pittsburgher. It has always excited me.

This was a recent Tuesday evening, and I was making good on a promise to take my wife Kathleen on a cruise to celebrate our 25th wedding anniversary. It was the barbecued chicken and ribs dinner special.

It was about a month early — August 12 is the official date — but better early than late, or never. I thought it was romantic because we had our first date, in November of 1966, aboard the original Gateway Clipper. We danced to the music of Harold "Mr. Trombone" Betters and his band ("Rambunctious") after a Steelers' home football game. Baldy Regan, the unofficial Mayor of the North Side, sponsored the cruise.

It doesn't seem that long ago.

This time we had our daughters Sarah and Rebecca, and their friends, Kara and Dana Pociask, four teenagers, with us. We pointed out places that had meaning from our past. As I kept pulling out dollar bills to buy one soft drink after another for our party, Kathie complained, "This is costing us more than our honeymoon."

How true. We didn't have much money when we got married, and Kathie had a new job at Presbyterian-University Hospital. She had to report to work in a couple of days, so we just drove across Pennsylvania and stopped wherever we saw a nice motel with a newsstand in front of it.

One of our overnight stops was in gorgeous Gas, Pa. I didn't realize that was the name of the town until I was paying the bill at the front desk the next morning, otherwise I would have moved on to a more romantic-sounding site. Somehow it all worked out for the best, and one of these days I am going to buy Kathie the engagement ring I promised to get her some day.

We were with good friends from our Upper St. Clair-Bethel Park Rotary Club on the cruise, so we had 50 or 60 familiar faces and a few hundred other strangers there to celebrate at our anniversary party. None of them was aware of what we were celebrating, but it was a nice, not-too-expensive reception, just the same.

As we cruised up and down the Monongahela, the Allegheny and the Ohio it was good to see that Pittsburgh's leaders are doing so much more to take advantage of the rivers and the shorelines.

Down the Ohio, I saw the ominous walls of Western Penitentiary, and that brought back a memory that pre-dated meeting Kathie.

It brought back the summer of '62. I won a Wall Street Journal Scholarship and had an opportunity to have a summer internship at *The Pittsburgh Press*. I was working on the city-side news desk.

One of the highlights of that summer experience was covering a riot at Western Penitentiary. It lasted a whole week, and I had a front-page byline just as long. It was the lead story all week. I spent a week as a sentry sitting atop a warehouse across the street from the penitentiary, with a view of the yard and water tower where the protesting prisoners had climbed and remained until the warden would hear their complaints.

John Place was the re-write man on the desk in those days. He was so quick, and he wrote with such clarity and economy, and we had some interesting exchanges as I described to him over the telephone some of the things that were going on up on the water tower.

When I bumped into Place years after at Atria's Restaurant & Tavern, when he was living in retirement in a nearby apartment complex, we would laugh about that week at the penitentiary. It was as close as I came to making good on the prediction of the Sisters of Charity that someday I would end up in a penitentiary.

That summer was a terrific experience and reinforced my belief that I wanted to be a newspaperman. One of my assignments that summer was to be an observer at the autopsy of a woman who was found dead on a street in Pittsburgh.

I also remember that one of Kathie's classmates in the School of Social Work lived in Woods Run near the prison. She and Kathie went on a short vacation trip to Miami and when I picked them up at the airport I realized how much I had missed Kathie. I asked her to marry me a day later. I'm glad that Kathie and I go back to those boats where it all began. It's been a wonderful journey, or as they might say, it's been a real trip.

As we went through the parking lot, we passed the Iron City Amphitheater. We could hear Willie Nelson singing "On the Road Again." We peeked through the fences to get a better look at one of my favorite singers, but someone I've lost a great deal of respect for because he didn't pay his taxes. If I had done what he did I would have ended up in a cell in Western Penitentiary.

> **"If you only have one smile in you, give it to the people you love."**
> **— Maya Angelou**

There will be rainy days in college, too

August 26, 1992

I wanted our daughter Sarah to get some highway driving time, so I let her take the wheel of our car when we entered West Virginia at its southern end. She and three of her girl friends had wanted to drive to an amusement park in Ohio this summer for sort of a pre-college weekend together, but had to scratch their plans when they discovered that none of them had ever driven on a turnpike.

I felt badly about that, in a way. There was a void in Sarah's driver education, and I didn't want that to happen again. She had worked hard and deserved a fun break with her friends. Sarah is a conscientious driver. She's put a few scratches on my bumpers from faulty parking efforts, but she tends to business when she is driving on the road. She was doing just fine, despite some unsolicited backseat assistance from her sister Rebecca and their mother.

I was a calm co-pilot, really, offering a word of advice about how to steer through this steep curve, or what to do in a tunnel. I was the one who taught her how to drive. None of us knows everything about driving a car. It's a demanding challenge. It started to rain. My first inclination was to instruct Sarah to pull off the road and let me drive. After all, rain changes the game considerably. I would feel more comfortable if I were driving in the rain. I am a more experienced driver. But I thought better of that notion. After all, it's going to rain some time when she's driving and I'm not there, and she has to get some experience at driving in the rain.

Better she do it when I was there and could offer some advice. Then she would feel more confident when she was on her own. And she was doing just fine. I told her to slow down a little on the curves, not to use cruise control when the road is wet, things like that. Then it started to rain harder. Only now we were coming down a mountainside. The shoulder of the road was very narrow, and there was nowhere to get off the road that seemed safe. And it started to pour. For awhile, I felt as if we were driving under Niagara Falls. Instead, we were on an especially steep slope heading down toward Cheat Lake. I began wishing we had pulled off the road a little earlier.

Rebecca and Kathie couldn't see the road at all from the back seat, and both started getting frightened. They also started hollering for us to pull off the road. Sarah was scared, I knew. The shouting only scared her more. I was concerned.

I told her to put on her blinking lights so any traffic behind us would know that we were going slower than the speed limit. Finally, I spotted a place where I thought we could pull off, and told Sarah to do so. She didn't do it quickly enough to suit me, so I urged her to do it faster. I didn't want us getting rear-ended by a truck. There was urgency in my voice, and I am sure it spooked her.

The rain slowed and I switched seats with Sarah. I could tell she was visibly shaken by the experience. As I write this, it all comes back to me, and it was a scary situation, indeed. After I took the wheel, we went up a highway about a half-mile and we saw a car dangling from the top of a high medial strip. It had been in a chain-reaction collision.

It only pointed out how dangerous that stretch of road had been during that downpour. That could have been us.

I told Sarah she would never forget that scary experience. It would stay with her the rest of her life. I had a similar scary near-miss with a disaster during my college days at Pitt. I drove to Penn State with Bob Smizik, a fellow sportswriter on *The Pitt News*, for a championship wrestling tournament. It had been snowing all day.

En route, we nearly slid under the back of a truck in a two-week-old Volkswagen Bug while traveling down a steep icy incline near Altoona. Later, we were in an accident, a fender-bender. But the near-miss was scarier than the accident. Seems to me like most of my near-misses and accidents happened in my high school and college days. We all feel pain in our hearts when we hear of an auto accident that claims the lives or severely injures young people. It prompts lectures on safety to our kids, who don't want to hear about it. They know better.

The next time Sarah finds herself in a downpour she will know that it's best to seek a safe spot before it gets worse. So will I. It was unfair to allow her to continue driving when the downpour worsened. She wasn't ready for it. If I had been driving, getting off the road and waiting for the rainfall to let up would have been the best bet.

We were coming home from Charlottesville, Virginia that day of the downpour. That is where Sarah is going to school on August 29, at the University of Virginia. She had an opportunity to show her mother and sister the school.

She had her dorm room assignment, so they were able to check out where she will be living this year. It's nice and it's convenient to the cafeteria. We can picture the place when we think of her this autumn and winter, and wonder how she is doing. That is comforting. But we will still miss her. If she's driving a car, I won't be there to steer her the right way.

Sarah and Rebecca flank their cousin's Airedale, Sophie, during visit to Churchman home in Raleigh, North Carolina.

It's difficult to say goodbye
in many ways

September 16, 1992

Our daughter Sarah sounds so excited when she calls at night to tell us about her latest adventures at the University of Virginia. She has been there a few weeks now, and she is still as smitten with the school as when we first visited it this past spring.

She just loves it. She is excited about everything, and she sounds so good on the telephone. I envy her this period in her life. I spoke to her on the eve of Virginia's season-opening football game at home with Maryland, and she was really looking forward to it.

Taking Sarah off to school the final weekend in August turned out not to be as difficult as I thought it would be. She was ready, and she had prepared us well for her departure.

It was much more difficult two years earlier when we took her to a summer music camp at Chautauqua, New York, because that was the first time she was away from home for an extended period. That was rough.

It was easier the following summer when we dropped her off at George Washington University, just down the street from The White House, and right smack in the middle of D.C. Somehow that seemed okay, too.

Those two summer experiences prepared her and us for this off-to-college challenge. What hurts some parents the most about their kids going off to college is that it sets in motion a chain of events, and that they may never return home, except for too-brief visits, ever again.

Kathie and I liked what we saw on our second visit to the University of Virginia. The freshman class was an attractive bunch. We didn't see anybody who looked bizarre, or who had a full body tattoo, or red or green hair, or crazy outfits, which is the case at a lot of colleges these days.

They seemed like a conservative class, the kind parents appreciate. Sarah seemed like she was making friends fast. She thought there were a lot of cute guys; I thought there were a lot of cute girls, or young women.

She successfully auditioned for the school/community orchestra, and she signed up for the yearbook, and to tutor kids three hours a week through a Charlottesville church. She's got the kind of class schedule I'd have choked on. I thought she had a full plate, but she spoke of adding another subject. I winced at the thought.

I wanted to take pictures of Sarah and her roommate, a young woman from Florida named Jenna, and all their suitemates. Sarah just stared at me, the way kids stare at parents when they wish you would disappear.

Jenna's mother said, "She's the last of my four to go to college. It's like I have a hole in my heart." I knew the feeling. I wanted to take pictures every time Sarah moved or spoke to another student that day we dropped her off for the start of a new chapter in her life, and in our lives. I wanted to capture the moment, you know.

Each time she walked the other way, no matter the reason, I snapped a shot of her. It was to capture her going in a different direction, I suppose. She told her mother and me that we always stay too long at such departures, and we did our best not to be too maudlin.

College campuses don't come much prettier than the University of Virginia. Tradition is important there. They want you to believe the school's founder Thomas Jefferson is still strolling the grounds. The first time I was there I listened to a choir song on the school's famous lawn. It seemed real old-fashioned.

There was more of the same this time when a group of girls who sing in an a cappella choir came by and sang for the campus newcomers as they took their furniture and wares into their dormitory rooms. It's great atmosphere.

One of Sarah's friends from Upper St. Clair High School, Christy O'Neill, who had already started her freshman year at nearby University of Richmond, sent her the first post card she received at her new address. They hope to get together this fall.

A few days later, Sarah heard from her friend, Kara Pociask, who was the last of her friends to go off to school. Kara was bound for Princeton. Another Kara, Kara Spak, had written earlier from Notre Dame, telling how much she missed all her friends, already.

These girls spent so much time together in the last days of August, as if they wanted to bond forever, that someone suggested they might have been happier if they had all gone off to Penn State together.

Colleges are special places. It's a special time in one's life. It's to be enjoyed to the fullest. We will miss her dearly, but we're happy that she is away at school. The last picture I shot showed Sarah walking down a grassy knoll in the midst of many of her classmates. They were going off to dinner together. I snapped that picture twice, just for good measure.

Sarah, as budding four-year-old artist at pre-school class on Long Island, shows off her latest work.

Best present delivered in the mail

December 30, 1992

I received a beautiful, heart-warming letter for Christmas. It may have been the best holiday present of all. It was not the form kind of catching-up-at-Christmas epistle I wrote to send out with cards for family and friends. It was a personal letter, a hand-written letter, and so legible. The handwriting reminded me of my mother's. Such letters have become a lost art.

It was from a woman named Margaret Lee. She was my nurse when I was born 50 years ago at Mercy Hospital. Her name was Peg Shea. She and my mother have written to each other every Christmas since then, and sometimes in between. They have been annual pen pals for 50 years.

They have never seen each other since that stay in the summer of '42 at Mercy Hospital. This has always been a source of amazement to me. Margaret Lee lives in Carlisle and, of course, that is in central Pennsylvania. There has always been talk about getting together, but it has never happened.

I have driven through Carlisle on occasion, always in a hurry, and I have never stopped to see Margaret Lee. Maybe there was fear of spoiling a good thing. This was only the second time I have received a letter from Margaret Lee. This year's was much more personal than last year's.

She has written me each of the last two years while ordering a copy of books about the Pittsburgh Steelers. She shares in my pride over their publication. She has a grandson out in the state of Washington named Ted, who is 16, an 11th grader, and interested in journalism, and she has had me sign a book for him.

She reported proudly that he is the Managing Editor (she spelled it with capital letters) of his high school newspaper. "He puts much time at it and loves it," she wrote. "Incidentally, the paper is ranked very high in the state and throughout the country. I knew he'd love to have his book autographed to him." She writes just like my mother.

I have always wondered what happened at Mercy Hospital that she and my mother formed this life-long attachment. How did they make such a lasting connection? It has long fascinated me. This woman gave me my middle name. It is Patrick. My full name is James Patrick O'Brien. For the record, I am Irish. When I was born in 1942 there was a popular movie out called "Rockne of Notre Dame," about the Fighting Irish football team, and it starred Pat O'Brien. Ronald Regan played George Gipp in the movie.

So my nurse at Mercy Hospital, who took a special liking to me as a newborn, dubbed me Pat, and apparently carried me around the maternity ward a lot. I'm glad she didn't call me Ron. My mother had no choice. She called me Pat, too.

In her most recent letter, Margaret Lee gave me some insight into her special relationship with my mother. My mother celebrated her 86th birthday this Christmas Eve. She was 35 when I was born. I was her fourth child. We were all born in a sequence in which the baby came five years after the previous baby. My oldest brother, Richard, turned 65 this year. My sister Carole turned 60. My brother Dan would have been 55. I am 50. It was a difficult year for milestones in our family.

"My friendship with your mother came at a time in my life when I had graduated from the Mercy School of Nursing in October, 1941," wrote Margaret Lee in her recent letter, "and rode back in the ambulance to my home in South Ford, Pennsylvania, with my mother who had pancreatic cancer. I cared for her till she died May 1, 1942.

"The nuns then called me and asked me if I'd come back to Mercy and set up a Newborn Nursery system (as I had suggested at the end of my student training there in obstetrics). I did so, but just for a short period as I was to enter the military service as a nurse.

"I had many wonderful patients when I was the head of the Nurseries, but your mother was especially kind to me. I had lost my father at age 11, so I was really on my own."

Now comes my favorite line — my mother hasn't been lying to me all these years after all — in the letter. "Then, too, you really were a beautiful baby and I fussed over you. I got in problems with the nun there in obstetrics because she didn't like big babies."

I weighed in at eight pounds ten ounces. Imagine a nun not liking big babies. Now I also understand why I always had such difficulty with nuns throughout my grade-school career. She wanted to beat the extra weight off me.

"Anyway," Margaret Lee continued in her letter, "your mother corresponded with me while I was in the military service in the South Pacific, and we continued on during the rest of our lives. She's a great lady."

I choked a little on that last line when I originally read the letter and, darn it, I'm doing it again as I write this column. Margaret Lee also let me know she is getting around much better now, and resuming many of her former activities, since getting a knee replacement. It was a problem caused, no doubt, by her proclivity for carrying heavy babies around when she was a nurse.

"Mercy Hospital has sent out information about the 100th anniversary of its nursing school in 1992, and plans a celebration April 30 and May 1 of 1993. I do hope I can attend and, hopefully, see your mother and also you."

That's great. I always like it when my mother has important dates on her calendar for special events. She would never miss a good party.

Saying goodbye to a barbecue grill

April 21, 1993

I never thought I would have such a difficult time saying goodbye to a gas barbecue grill. Our barbecue grill gave out on us on a recent weekend. It couldn't take the heat anymore. Kathie called it "a meltdown." She told me it was time to toss it out.

The instrument panel, where you adjust the flame and so forth, finally fried itself beyond repair and recognition. I had scorched it pretty good myself last summer, turning the heat up too high, and taking my eye off it for too long.

It melted half of one of the dials. But I was able to make some adjustments and it still worked, so we went on with our summer cookouts. It didn't look good, but the chicken, hot dogs, hamburgers and steaks that came off it still tasted terrific. I didn't light it the last time. For some reason, I declined when Kathie asked me to fire up the grill. Maybe I had a premonition or something. "You do it," I urged her.

A half-hour later, she came to me with the bad news. I went out on the side porch and saw that the dials, some screws, and part of a wire, had all dropped onto the floor of the porch. The barbecue grill had expired.

As I was detaching the propane tank, and getting the grill ready for the garbage collector, I started thinking about the times we'd prepared meals on it. I started thinking about summer outings with Kathie and the kids, Sarah and Rebecca, and some good memories.

I didn't light that barbecue grill the first time, either. I asked a woman who lived next door to do it. I had never started a gas grill before and, frankly, had a healthy (or unhealthy) fear of it.

I had managed to get a model that was already assembled at the Busy Beaver Building Center at South Hills Village, advising the clerk that I wouldn't buy a car if I had to assemble it myself. That was five or six years ago. The neighbor didn't know it, but I moved back a few steps when she stuck a miniature flame-thrower into its bowels to light the gas. My dad was timid when it came time to lighting our gas stove, or changing a fuse, or changing a fluorescent bulb in a lighting fixture. My mother had to handle those tasks. So I blame my dad for my cowardice. It's in the genes. My dad was also a softie when it came to kids. I felt bad when I was wheeling the barbecue grill to the bottom of the driveway, where I had already placed several boxes and bags of garbage for a weekly pick-up. I was hoping someone, maybe a handyman, would come by and take it before the garbage collectors came.

The barbecue grill had become a fixture on our side porch, a fixture in our family life, and I didn't want to let go of it. It reminded me of what it was like when I had to take down the swing set, rusty as it had become, when the girls had outgrown it. Or replacing couches in our family room when they'd gotten a little threadbare.

Maybe the barbecue grill was simply a symbol of the change that has been taking place at our house. Too much change. I don't handle change as well as I once did. I heard the narrator in a TV movie recently say, "I used to take pride in looking forward, and now I find myself always looking backward." It felt familiar. On the Tuesday morning when our garbage is collected, I found some old papers I decided I no longer needed. So I filled up a box, and took it to the bottom of the driveway.

My timing was terrible. The men had already picked up the barbecue grill and tossed it into the belly of the garbage truck. I had to chase after the garbage truck to give the men the bag.

As I did, I spotted my grill. It was lying in garbage. In garbage! I could see some gleaming grillwork, and wondered whether I should have hung onto that, for some possible use when I got my new grill.

I hated the idea of my barbecue grill going to join Jimmy Hoffa in some landfill. But the blue truck of the South Hills Disposal Company drove off before I could read the phone number on its side.

Rebecca and Sarah help their father, sort of, to rake leaves in backyard.

Driving Miss Rebecca
was a real challenge

June 2, 1993

I was painting a panel on my garage door, doing my best to touch up a tear in the exterior. I was painting it with North Carolina blue enamel and hoping that what I was doing would blend in with the rest of the door. So no one would notice the splinters.

And I thought about how difficult it was to teach my daughter Rebecca how to drive. I knew it was going to be difficult to teach her how to drive. I knew it the day she was born on May 7, 1977.

She came into this world beet-red and protesting. And she has been protesting ever since, or so it seems anyhow. I think she was unhappy that I was watching when she came into this world.

Rebecca has been taking me on an emotional roller coaster ride ever since. I love her dearly, but she doesn't make it easy. She doesn't take instruction well. "She's just like you, that's why," says Kathie, her mother and my wife, in that order, to build my confidence.

Rebecca could not wait to get rolling. No sooner had she turned 16 than she was in a hurry to qualify for this year's Indy 500. I tried to tell her she had to learn how to crawl before she could learn how to walk and how she had to learn how to walk before she could run. Turn the record off, Dad, she said in her own beloved way. "Don't be so gay," she said, invoking one of her favorite put-downs.

We even had a difficult time getting her a learner's permit. That was my fault. She told me she would need her birth certificate and her social security card when we went to the driver's testing station in Washington. I couldn't find her card, but I had her number. Surely, that would suffice.

"You can't take your test today," the officer said sternly, rejecting Rebecca's bid to hit the open road. The officer reminded me of officers I'd encountered in the U.S. Army. Everything by the book.

We returned the next day, with her official social security card, and Rebecca passed her written examination with flying colors. She had studied the rules of the road well. The next day we were going to go out together in my car for her first behind-the-wheel experience. Rebecca asked me to back the car out of the garage and down the driveway, admitting she wasn't ready to do that just yet.

After all, she had been in a car a few days earlier when the mother of her best friend managed to wipe out our mailbox. Her husband replaced it with a new one the next day, so we came out of that miscue ahead of the game. Rebecca went to the bottom of the driveway and stood ready to replace me at the wheel. "Not so fast," I told her. "You're not going to start out by driving through our neighborhood." Rebecca, of course, was not ready for that.

I took her to the empty parking lot at Westminster Presbyterian Church, which is laid out a lot like the area where she will eventually take her driver's test. She protested. The area was too confining, the turns too tight. It was boring. I saw it as safe.

I remembered I had taken my first few turns at the wheel of an auto on a football field with my brother Dan, and in a cemetery with my Uncle Everett Burns. "You can't kill anyone here," my Uncle Everett explained.

My sentiments exactly. I relented to Rebecca's protest, and took her for a spin behind her high school. That was a big mistake. She clipped a few curbs when she got nervous about oncoming traffic. When she wrenched a tire against a curb, I had her get out of the car to check out what the tire looks like when it's jammed against a curb, and how the whitewall stripe has a seizure.

"It's better to hit a curb than a car," she said in her defense. How can you argue with such logic? Before she struck the curb, she had been zeroing in, like a heat-seeking missile, on a man and his dog. The man was allowing his dog to do something on a patch of grass where the school kids play. So if Rebecca had wiped them out, at least it would have been justifiable homicide.

Needless to say, our first day out didn't go well. Rebecca wasn't happy with me and I wasn't happy with her. I kissed her the next morning, told her I still loved her, and that I would take her out again that evening. Our second session went much better, without incident. This time we tooled around the parking lot, a lot more spacious than the Westminster one, behind St. John Capistran Church at the other end of Upper St. Clair. She did well.

She needed to learn how a car responds to your foot on the gas pedal or the brake pedal, how much it turns when you twist the wheel, basic stuff like that. Stuff that has to be mastered before you start driving on real roads. Because we don't have sidewalks in our neighborhood she didn't have any experience at steering kids' cars or bikes. Again, my fault.

Rebecca thought it was stupid. None of her friends had to do that. It was dumb. Left unsaid, I was a dumb dad. The next day I borrowed my wife's car, a Jeep Wagoneer, because I needed to pick up a billboard that day that would not fit into my car trunk. It's not as powerful as my car, and I thought it would be easier for Rebecca to control.

I raised the rear lift gate to remove the billboard, but forgot to lower it. With Rebecca riding shotgun, I got into the car and backed it out of the garage. I had managed to press the gizmo that raises the garage door overhead. But the rear lift gate, which I had failed to lower, struck the bottom panel of the raised garage door and I felt real resistance to my attempt to back out onto the driveway. I felt so stupid. So dumb.

I had damaged the garage door. It came off the tracks. Kathie would be coming home in five to ten minutes. Then I would really feel dumb. Kathie would see to that. Fortunately, Kathie's car wasn't damaged.

When Terry Wright, a handsome young man, arrived from Wright's Garage Door Service, he smiled and said, "Hi, Mr. O'Brien. Is this going to be a column?" Sure, why not? Rebecca will be a good driver someday. And she will never let me forget about my auto accident in our garage.

Rebecca learns to "drive" a horse at Thomas farm in New York. Somehow that seemed easier than teaching her how to drive an automobile.

Nancy is both a hair stylist and a psychiatrist

June 30, 1993

I have been getting my hair cut for the past 14 years by one woman, a hair stylist named Nancy Christensen Cardiello. My hair was mostly dark brown when I began going to her for my monthly grooming, and now it's mostly gray.

She was working at Your Father's Mustache in South Hills Village when she first started cutting my hair, and I followed her to The Hair House, near the Lebanon Shops on Mt. Lebanon Boulevard, and now Bellingham's Studio of Hair Design on Painters Run Road in Upper St. Clair.

I don't like change, and she always stayed within a reasonable distance of my home and, frankly, I didn't want to start all over again with a new barber or hair stylist. The same goes for my dentist.

Besides, she has also been my dime-store psychiatrist and family counselor, and I didn't want to go back to the beginning with my stories if someone else were to assume her tasks.

I always thought her fee was a little steep — it's $17 now — but that's because I can't forget that I used to get my hair cut as a little kid for fifty cents. But when I considered what it would cost to go to a regular psychiatrist, I figured I was getting my money's worth.

It took President Clinton and an inflamed larynx to make me really appreciate Nancy. You will recall the flap President Clinton created when the word got out that he had gotten a $200 haircut by Christopher of Beverly Hills aboard Air Force One, closing off a couple of runways at the airport in Los Angeles. That's nearly a year's worth of haircuts from Christensen-Cardiello of Bellingham's.

When I went to see Nancy for my May haircut, I learned that she had an inflamed larynx — she wrote this information on an erasable pad for me — and she was under doctor's orders not to talk for two weeks.

I hated having my hair cut by Nancy with no conversation coming from her mouth. I felt cheated. I thought I was really getting clipped. I thought I was getting my hair cut by Chico Marx or Marcel Marceau. I could see her motions in the mirror, but it wasn't the same. I am not good at reading lips when she tried to mouth a few remarks. I gave her only a $2 tip instead of the usual $3 tip.

I missed the latest news Nancy had to offer. I missed her showing me pictures of her daughters and grandchild, and catching me up on their recent activities. I missed hearing what she thought about what I had to say. Plus, while I waited, I got to glean the latest headlines in all the sensational tabloids, in the reception area. You can't get that stuff in our local library.

Nancy is a nice person. She is generally pleasant, bright-eyed, animated in her conversation. She cares about her kids. She has a good sense of humor. And, for what it's worth, I like the way she cuts my hair.

She is the mother of two girls, Dana, who's 28, and Darlene, who's 25. Dana is off in Japan for a second time with a theatrical dance troupe from Disney World in Orlando, where she has been living in recent years. Darlene lives in Finleyville. She has a five-year-old son, Richard, who is the apple of Nancy's blue-green eyes.

"I love to talk to Richard," says Nancy. "He is older than his years."

There's a three-year age difference between Nancy's daughters, and a three-and-a-half year difference between my daughters, Sarah, 19, and Rebecca, 16. So Nancy had an awareness of what life was like for such girls, and gave me lots of good tips about child-rearing. She never pretended she was an expert, but she openly shared her sentiments on the subject. She prepared me for what was ahead.

Nancy's daughters delighted her at times, and they frustrated her at times, but I always had the feeling that she would go to war on behalf of either of them. I have always been close to my barbers, right from the beginning, so Nancy was no exception.

As a boy, I lived next door to a duplex where two brothers — both barbers — were married to two sisters and lived in adjoining quarters. That was Tony and Joe Figoli. A third sister, who lived a block away, was also married to a barber named Frank Marone. His son, Frank Jr., was also a barber and he worked for Joe Figoli.

I still run into Frank Jr. from time to time at malls in the South Hills.

I remember how all the children and grandchildren used to visit our next-door neighbors on Sunday, and how they all got free haircuts on the backporch. Talk about a busman's holiday.

Later on, my brother and I started visiting the Vavro Brothers, about a half-mile down the same stretch, Second Avenue in Hazelwood, to get our hair cuts. Bob, Joe and Eddie Vavro followed in their father's footsteps and had the most popular barber shop in Hazelwood.

They were all talkers. They were into sports and local gossip. They told tales of the latest news in town with great excitement and gestures. They were entertainers as well as barbers, especially Joe, who now resides in Bethel Park, but still runs the barber shop on Second Avenue. Eddie has a place Downtown in the basement of the U.S. Steel Tower and Bob has become a top-level union official.

They bred me to enjoy a good conversation while I was sitting in a barber's chair. Joe used to crack me up with blow-by-blow descriptions of brawls involving the principals at a recent wedding reception. He told great stories.

I went back to see Nancy earlier this month. Her voice was back. She was her old self. I tipped her an extra dollar to make up for what I had shortchanged her the month before. Nancy had stored up two months' worth of news to share with me. President Clinton could learn something from her.

Nancy is now a hair stylist at Bellingham's at the Great Southern Shopping Center in Bridgeville, Pa. Nancy has been cutting my hair for more than 25 years. Joe Vavro has a barber shop-hair styling salon on Interboro Avenue in Lincoln Place. Brother Eddie is still at the U.S. Steel Tower and Bob is retired.

Hair stylist Nancy Cardiello is flanked by her daughters, left to right, Dana Lynn, and Darlene Susan.

Rebecca, Sarah, Kathie and Jim

Kathie, Sarah and Rebecca in earlier days

The summer all my girls went to work

September 29, 1993

I learned something special this summer about my daughters. They like to work. They both went to work for the first time in their young lives and they liked it. They truly enjoyed their jobs. It's a good start.

They like working outside the home more than they have ever liked working at home.

They like earning their own money. It is more appreciated and different from an allowance.

They spend the money they make much more slowly than they spend the money their parents make. They bank their checks as quickly as they get them. It's a family tradition.

A $6 ticket for a movie is much more expensive to them now, when they have to work almost an hour and half to get the money for it. A $28 ticket for a Penguins game is out of sight when they consider it's a day's work.

Yes, this was a significant summer at our home.

Rebecca celebrated her Sweet 16 birthday at the beginning of the summer and her sister Sarah celebrated her 20th birthday at the end of the summer. I can't believe my girls are 16 and 20.

It gave me pause for thought. It is difficult to comprehend that it was 20 years ago that I first saw Sarah, in an incubator, just as a precaution, at a hospital on Long Island. It was Mercy Hospital in Rockville Centre. I am writing this column on her birthday. She is away at school, a sophomore at the University of Virginia, and we will have to wait two weeks to visit her to properly mark the occasion in Charlottesville.

Today, she seems farther away from home than usual.

Rebecca is so eager to begin driving a car on her own. I worry whenever she is in a car, no matter who is doing the driving. Sometimes I wish they were both still in incubators, just as a precaution.

Both of them had two jobs this summer. They grew up considerably during the school break. Both made new friends.

Rebecca has become a hostess at Eat'n Park Restaurant at South Hills Village, where our family has eaten so often through the years. She's also worked an eight-hour shift one day a week as a volunteer at Allegheny General Hospital.

She took advantage of the teachers' strike at Upper St. Clair High School, where she is a junior this year, to work more day shifts through September. "If this keeps up," she said in jest, "I'll be rich."

Sarah worked 40 hours or more each week as a student research intern at Allegheny General Neuropsychiatric Institute (ANI) out in Oakdale. It was a great internship. It was a two-month internship, but Sarah continued to report to work on occasion even when she was no longer being paid to do so simply because she enjoyed it, and felt she was learning a great deal. She wants to return there next summer.

She was lucky that the staff, starting with Dr. Paul Nussbaum, was all eager to spend personal time with her, to teach her, to encourage her, to nourish an interest in what they were doing to help patients. Good doctors and good teachers do that. They involved her in all facets of their program, and she had a lot of hands-on interaction with everyone at the hospital.

Sarah also worked from 16 to 21 hours a week as a sales clerk at Horne's at South Hills Village. Like her sister, she learned how to use a cash register, how to serve and please customers, how to handle supervision, criticism, complaints, etc., and keep smiling.

Our girls have a work heritage. Their mother and their grandmothers all worked in department stores. Their mother just marked her 18-month anniversary as a social worker in the oncology unit at Allegheny General Hospital. That is both a demanding and a rewarding job. It's more like a mission. Altogether, their mother has been working nearly two years outside our home.

Kathie went to work at Kaufmann's for the holiday season shortly after I lost a job as editor of *Street & Smith's Basketball Yearbook* in November of 1992. She had a job within three days. She never laid a guilt trip on me. Her working provided a bridge for me to start writing and publishing books on my own. She enabled me to do something I wanted to do, but could not have afforded to do without her help.

She has been working over 26 years in our home. She continues to keep everything clean and to wash and iron everyone's clothes. Rebecca's green and white uniform, for instance, has to be laundered daily. That is a house rule, or requirement, at Eat'n Park, you might be pleased to know.

So all the women in our house were working this year. They all have a good work ethic. They come by it honestly. Work was valued in our families. Their bloodlines go back to coal miners, steel mill workers, railroaders, street car motormen, and women who worked in cafeterias and behind counters in State Stores and Murphy's 5 & 10 stores.

Their grandparents remember The Great Depression only too well. I recall hearing stories about how my mother and father knocked on doors in their neighborhood to work, any kind of work, to pay for the rent and groceries during that difficult period when few had real jobs.

Once Kathie and I were in school, our mothers went off to work, to help pay the bills. They didn't want to owe anybody any money. They wouldn't have considered leaving us with anyone else before we were in school.

None of the women in my house missed a day of work this summer. They have the right stuff. They get to work on time. They are reliable and responsible. They have good attitudes.

They have been taught that a job is to be enjoyed, and to be cherished. Nobody owes you a job. Nobody owes you security. Anybody who has given you a job has done you a favor. It's not your job; it's their job. So just say "Thank you," and get to work.

Spending a week at the beach in North Carolina put smiles on the faces of O'Brien family.

They really were good ol' boys

I still question my judgment when I reflect on this story. Was I too trusting? I was still picking up hitchhikers into my mid-40s, so maybe I was simply stupid.

October 13, 1993

I shudder when I think of how things could have gone even more wrong. Something bad could have happened. It restores my faith in my fellow man that things turned out as well as they did. There are still Good Samaritans out there. There are still some trustworthy people. And they have different faces. We needed help and some people came to our rescue.

My wife Kathie and I, and our daughter, Rebecca, were visiting Virginia at the outset of October. We were going to check out James Madison University in Harrisonburg as Rebecca begins her search for a college to attend two years down the road. And we were going to see Sarah, our older daughter, who was playing her cello in weekend concert performances by the Charlottesville and University Symphony Orchestra.

I thought I had done my best to get my automobile in order for the trip. After all, I had gotten a new transmission the week before, a new set of brakes for the front wheels, new tires on the front wheels, and had everything under the hood checked out at Chuck's Auto Service near my home before we departed. I always stopped there to get things checked out before I drove any long distance.

Even so, as we emerged from having lunch at KFC in Harrisonburg we discovered that we had a dead battery under the hood. It had fried somewhere along the highways from Pittsburgh. We were due to start our tour of the campus at James Madison in 15 minutes. Normally, we would have had time to spare to get there on time. But now we had a problem.

I saw two guys sitting in a pick-up truck three parking spaces away. It was one of those pick-up trucks that has been elevated with a lift kit, so you can see the rear axle housing and all sorts of springs in its underbelly. It's the kind of pick-up truck I hate. I usually make some snide remark whenever one passes me on the road. To me, they are a menace to the road, and make a statement about the sort of people who own them.

On the positive side, however, they normally indicate that the driver knows something about motor mechanics. Otherwise, they wouldn't fool around with a pick-up truck and customize it like that. The two men were eating fried chicken inside the cab. They had the windows up and they were listening to loud country music. It wasn't Garth Brooks or Billy Ray Cyrus, or anybody I would recognize, but real back-road country music. I had to rap hard on the window to get their attention.

They smiled, cracked the window, and they came over to my car, and checked out some things under the hood, and confirmed that my battery was, indeed, quite dead. They didn't have any jumper cables. They seemed friendly enough. Both of them had long sideburns, and certified southern accents. It's amazing to me how quickly the accents change when you head south from Pittsburgh. They continued to check this and that under the hood, and seemed determined to help us.

The two fellows in the pick-up truck offered a ride. "We can get you there," one of them volunteered. The two fellows who offered the ride looked a lot cleaner and friendlier than the two fellows who were preparing to tow my car back to their shop after we called Triple A.

"Do you think we'll be OK?" Kathie asked me.

"I think so," I said, not really giving it the thought it deserved. "They seem friendly enough."

90

I slipped Kathie a crisp $10 bill and told her to give it to them when she got to the JMU campus, something for their trouble. So Kathie climbed up in the pick-up truck, and Rebecca sat in her lap, and they left the parking lot. I looked at them as they left, and second-guessed myself for a moment.

Would I ever see them again? Would they be OK? I convinced myself that they would be all right. The guys I was with knew them well. Of course, I still don't know any of their names, except for Rick. He didn't have a last name, or many teeth for that matter. But he seemed to know his stuff about cars.

I needed a new battery, and I had to pay $30 for the towing, and $25 for the labor, and $86 for the battery. And it had to be cash. No checks or credit cards. I had only $102 in cash. Rick's friend, who was doing most of the work, and owned his own auto repair shop nearby but was helping Rick out this particular day, took me to a bank to get an advance on my Visa credit card. I didn't even know you could do that.

The guy ahead of me in the bank line was dressed like a cowboy, with a black hat, black blouse, and black jeans with a special white design stitching. He looked like Paladin. Remember Paladin — the TV bounty hunter played by Richard Boone?

The mechanics thought I might need a new alternator — it might have caused my battery to burn up — and that would have cost another $190. After checking the battery charge again, they decided I could get back to Pittsburgh OK. I drove to James Madison University and caught up with Kathie and Rebecca at an information session. We were relieved to see each other.

"We were quite a scene when we showed up in that jacked-up truck in the center of the campus, and climbed down for a tour," said Kathie. "Hopefully, the Dean of Admissions didn't see us arriving. The guys in the truck were nice guys. They wouldn't take any money. The guy said, 'Absolutely not.' They just wanted to help us."

Rebecca and Sarah

No nunsense with Sister Ann Patricia

January 8, 1994

A good teacher is to be treasured for a lifetime. So Sister Ann Patricia has always been close to my heart.

She was my teacher in seventh grade at St. Stephen's Grade School in Hazelwood, a once-proud mill town community at the southeast end of Pittsburgh. She was also my English teacher in eighth grade.

Sister Ann Patricia was a formidable figure in my youth. She was not to be messed with. She grew up in nearby West Homestead and knew how to deal with difficult students. She had a sharp tongue and a hard forehand. And a strong hug.

I will never forget her berating me in front of the entire class on one occasion. She got my attention and I got her point. She could hurt me more with a tongue-lashing than with a whip-lashing. And she knew it.

She loved sports and, down deep, I felt she loved me. At least, that's the way I felt. She would not put up with any nonsense, or nunsense. She helped me with my grammar, and encouraged me with my writing.

I thought she believed in me, and was behind me, just like my mother. She was one nun my mother could talk to without losing her patience. They were on the same page.

During November and December, Sister Ann Patricia came to my mind more than once. I thought about her again and several of the sisters I had at St. Stephen's when I went to the movie theater at The Galleria in Mt. Lebanon to see Whoopi Goldberg in *Sister Act II.*

93

I never had a nun who looked like or behaved like Whoopi. No nun ever inspired me to sing. In fact, one nun tapped me harshly on the forehead a few times with her baton during a rehearsal for our confirmation ceremony and told me I was not to sing in church. I was the only student singled out and instructed not to sing. I was that bad. I am still that bad. I still know the words to the songs we were to sing. They have been stuck in my mind ever since. "Holy God, we praise thy name . . . infinite thy vast domain."

I was also banished from the class to become an altar boy, and still remember some of the Latin I learned in vain. "Dominus vobiscum, et cum spiritu tuo."

There were nuns who put large paper clips on my tongue to keep me from talking during class and I mean the large paper clips — the ones that snap shut like a mouse trap — and nuns who had me kneel on blackboard pointers.

Sister Mary Lucy, my fifth grade teacher, once stood midway between Francis "Deezer" Connelly and me and alternately struck him and me on the head with a window pusher, a lance-like tool as lethal as the ones used in jousting by Sir Lancelot of King Arthur's Court. Imagine what might happen to any teacher who tried that medieval torture today. We just thought it was another day at school.

As I saw it, detention was my last class of the day. My mother thought school lasted a half-hour longer than it really did. I enjoyed detention. All my best buddies were there to keep me company.

In November, as I was motoring one morning toward Monroeville, where I was to lecture several seventh grade classes at Gateway Middle School about writing and reading, I reflected on my days in seventh grade. What did I remember best about seventh grade?

I was traded in seventh grade. That's right. I started out the school year with a young nun, fresh out of school or the nunnery, who shall go unnamed here. She was thought by the principal, Sister Mary Barbara, to be too young to effectively deal with the likes of me.

So I was traded, sent across the hall on the third floor at St. Stephen's Grade School to the classroom presided over by Sister Ann Patricia. I no more than walked into Sister Ann Patricia's class than she put me on warning as to what was expected of me.

Through the years, I have poked fun at my nuns, and gotten cheap laughs at their expense. But, on reflection, I was lucky to have them as teachers.

They kept me in line and taught me a lot. I needed the discipline. I still do. As tough as they were, I never disliked them. They made my school days more interesting, more challenging. And I knew they prayed for me a lot.

My eighth grade teacher, Sister Mary Leo, told my mother that I was going to end up in Sing-Sing some day. So when I graduated from Pitt, my mother sent a graduation notice to Sister Mary Leo, and attached a note, "See, he didn't end up in Sing-Sing after all."

Myron Cope cautioned my mother not to be too premature in her comment. "He still has a shot at Sing-Sing," Cope told my mother.

I wasn't that fond of Sister Mary Leo, but I loved the rest of them: Sister Mary Thomas, Sister Macrina, Mrs. Kyle, Sister Marie Patrick, Sister Mary Lucy, Sister Mary Pius. Mary was obviously a popular name among nuns in those days.

Sister Macrina hung me from a coat hook in the robery, or cloakroom, by the straps of my leggings for making a smart aleck remark. When some of the girls teased me about wearing leggings, I snapped back at them, "My old lady made me wear them!"

When Sister Macrina heard me say that — those nuns could pick up such a remark from across the room — she seized me, and hung me up on a hook by the straps of those leggings. One of my cousins, Everett Burns, genuflected when he passed me in the cloakroom. He must have mistaken me for one of the Stations of the Cross. For the record, I never referred to my mother as "my old lady" ever again.

Sister Mary Pius made me her pet. She blamed the other students for getting me into trouble. She was a favorite, too. Sister Marie Patrick used to give me her copies of *Arizona Highways* magazine.

Sister Ann Patricia must have known I was thinking about her during the holidays. She always knew what I was thinking. She sent me a beautiful Christmas card, "I like your philosophy," she wrote. "I always knew you would reach your goal."

Sister Ann Patricia is 72. She retired two years ago after 18 years as the principal at St. Luke's in Carnegie. She said her health is so-so. She said Father Joseph Meenan, who officiated at my marriage to Kathie at St. Stephen's nearly 27 years ago, says Mass at St. Luke's. Father Meenan also officiated, along with Bishop Carroll, at my confirmation. That's the one where I wasn't allowed to sing the hymns I had memorized.

Everyone loses out today because teachers aren't permitted to hit or hug their students. They risk going to jail if they do either. "Don't touch them," they are told.

"I still hug them," said Sister Ann Patricia, in a bit of a confession. "Whatever we did, we thought it was the right thing to do. We really loved the kids. When they were hurting we were hurting."

She warned me not to work too hard, not to get stressed out. My mother was the only other woman on this earth who offered similar suggestions of concern. "Enjoy yourself," said Sister Ann Patricia at the end of our conversation. "I'll say a prayer for you and your family. God bless."

I got off the phone and just sat there for a moment.

"Nothing happens unless first a dream."
— Carl Sandburg

Worrying about the weather and the kids

January 26, 1994

I was shoveling snow at 7 a.m. on a Monday earlier this month. I was clearing the sidewalk and driveway outside my home. The snow was about four inches deep and was pure white. I was worrying about what it would be like at 7 a.m. the next day. That's when I was scheduled to drive my daughter Sarah and one of her classmates, Todd Melagari, back to school at the University of Virginia.

More snow and record low temperatures were on tap.

What would the roads be like? What would be the best route to take? Should I get new tires on my car? Hadn't I bought new tires earlier this summer? Should we wait till Wednesday to depart Pittsburgh for the trip to Charlottesville? What is wrong with me?

I am getting more like my mother every day. And that worries me.

My brother Dan traveled round the world in his job, to Japan and Australia and South Africa. My mother had a field day worrying about him.

At this time of year, I used to be jumping on and off airplanes every day or night. There were winters when I reported on the activities of pro basketball and pro hockey teams and would be emerging from steamy locker rooms to board airplanes in the worst weather on a daily basis.

One night it was Buffalo, the next night it was Boston, then Philadelphia, back to New York, off to Chicago, Detroit and Milwaukee, with maybe a stop in Indianapolis in between. My mother knew the weather conditions in every city where I was covering games. She would alert me in advance as to what I ought to wear when I went to Denver. Whatever Joe knows, Mary knows better.

The Steelers weren't as informed about weather conditions in cities where they were traveling. I used to tell my mother not to worry. I would kid her about her concern. What's to worry? That was my outlook. How come I have forgotten my spirit for travel in those days? Then again, earthquakes truly happened in California in those days, not in Reading, Pa. My wife Kathie recently admonished me. "For goodness sake, you're talking like your mother. Don't you remember when you were young? Would this weather have held you back?"

I had been expressing some concern about our daughters, Sarah and Rebecca, and their respective travel plans. We were in the midst of the first heavy snowfall of the winter, and the roads were bad, yet Rebecca was going out with some friends to a restaurant and to the movies, and I thought it would be wise for her to stay home. The roads were slippery.

I was already worrying about some travel plans Sarah had made. On the weekend before she would return to school after the semester break, she was scheduled to visit her girl friend Kara Pociask at Princeton.

In my bones then, I knew the weekend was going to turn up bad weather-wise. And it came up as cold and blustery as possible. The Sunday newspaper carried a banner headline heralding our town as Iceburgh rather than Pittsburgh. That was reassuring.

On the morning Sarah was scheduled to fly to Newark, I got up early and tuned in the weather channel. The reports sounded like they were coming from Siberia. I checked the weather reports on the radio. One story was about an airline accident from a year ago when a USAir plane slid off the runway at LaGuardia Airport in New York, injuring many of the passengers. Great! Just what I needed to reassure me.

Sarah went back and forth to Princeton with just an hour delay getting out of Pittsburgh. I visited my mother while Sarah was still at Princeton. As I was leaving my mother's apartment, she said, "Listen, I want you to do me a favor."

"What's that?" I said.

"Please call me as soon as you get in from Virginia," she said, blowing me a kiss because she had a cold. "Let me know when you get home."

Sarah and Rebecca
play in snow
in front yard of
their new home
in Upper St. Clair.

It doesn't get any easier to swap cars

March 24, 1995

I sent Sarah back to school the other day with a new set of wheels. She was driving a shiny silver-blue four-door sedan that was 3-½ years old, but the four tires were all brand new. I insisted that the car dealer put new tires on it.

"They're fair to middlin'," the car salesman had said of the four tires that were on the car when I first checked it over. "They're not bad."

"Would you want your son driving back and forth to college on them?" I asked. He agreed to put on a new set of tires.

Sarah was thrilled to find a new car in the driveway when she came home from school for a weeklong (and too short) spring break. Her sister Rebecca had told her the car was a "baby blue" one, as sort of a putdown, so she was pleased to see that it was more of a silver-blue number. It was clean as can be, especially under the hood, as if that mattered to Sarah.

And it had a "new car smell" about it. I think you can buy that in auto parts and accessories stores.

It was a 1991 Toyota Corolla with 43,000 miles on it, and 17,000 miles or a year-and-a-half warranty remaining. Sarah had a year-and-a-half to go at the University of Virginia — that's hard to believe — and I'll be happier if she gets through graduate school with it.

It wasn't that difficult to buy this car. I thought I got lucky. But it was difficult to trade in a car to get it.

Kathie and I had come to love our 1986 Jeep Wagoneer Cherokee. We had it nearly ten years, and we had put 86,000 miles on it. It was really Kathie's car, but I always loved to drive it. I liked sitting up high, I liked the feel of it, the bus driver's view, the feeling of safety. It was also great for hauling things.

It was the second time in six months we had to give up the ghost on cars we'd had for nearly ten years. In fact, I learned when I traded in the Wagoneer that we had traded in a ten-year-old Volvo sedan when we originally purchased it.

That tells what marriage did for me. I keep cars ten years now whereas I never owned a car outright before I got married nearly 28 years ago. When I was young and single, I bought $100 and $200 bombs. Back in the early '60s, I bought a black 1933 Plymouth because it looked like one of the cars in *The Untouchables*, but I had to give it up in less than a week because it had bad brakes.

I bought a Mercury bomb once in an alley somewhere in Beechview and I recall how my friends and I had to drag our sneakers on the road to get it to stop on a small slope. I went through a series of those two-week specials, perhaps the most expensive cars I ever owned.

I bought my first new car at a dealership on the suburban side of the Liberty Tunnels. It was a Volkswagen Beetle. Didn't everybody have one of those "Bugs" when they were in college back in the '60s?

It cost me about $5,000 and two weeks later I slid on a snow-covered road into an oncoming car traveling through the mountains to Penn State to see the Eastern Wrestling Championships. The damage was to the tune of $1,200. Later, I traded that in for a Karmann Ghia, a great looking car that had an Italian body and a German engine. It had an anthracite black body and pearl-white roof. It was a beauty. I took it to the World's Fair in New York. Twice.

Back then, I just made monthly payments. I'd get bored with the color after a year and trade it in for a new model.

> *"Everything in life is somewhere else and you get there in a car."*
> — E. B. White

Then I got married. Soon after, I owned my first car. It's been that way ever since. Kathie brought sanity and order to my life.

"She's the best thing that ever happened to you," my mother told me recently. "She settled you down."

I nearly chickened out on trading in the Wagoneer. It was part of the family. I felt like I was abandoning one of the kids at an orphanage.

At the last minute, I got cold feet and called friends for advice. "You've got to give up your love," said a friend who sells cars at a rival dealer, "and go with common sense."

Common sense? When I was checking out used cars, I came across a flaming red Alfa Romeo convertible. If I were a college kid, that would be the car for me. But, as the father of two daughters, I was looking for a surplus Army tank that gets 60 miles to a gallon of gas.

I settled for something that makes sense and something we could afford to buy for cash. Drive it in good health, Sarah.

Sarah and Rebecca relax in family room.

From Graduation Day to Father's Day

June 14, 1995

A good friend of mine, Stan Goldmann, told me something his father had told him. When the younger Goldmann graduated from high school, his father took him aside and said, "Your grandfather and I spent our lives building a good reputation for our family, and I don't want you to ever do anything to tarnish that."

Goldmann smiled at the recollection. "That has always been my guideline," he said.

Goldmann had invited me to lunch last week, and we got together at DeBlasio's Restaurant in Mt. Lebanon. Goldmann had retired a year earlier as president of Geyer Printing in Oakland, where all my books are printed. He now lives most of the time in Sanibel, Florida, and keeps a townhouse on Mt. Washington.

His comment was prompted by some thoughts I had offered about my dealings with my younger daughter, Rebecca, who works as a hostess and waitress at Eat'n Park Restaurant at South Hills Village.

She had turned 18 in May and was going to be graduated from Upper St. Clair High School that Sunday evening and was eager to steer her own course in life. In my opinion, Rebecca had confused her birthday with Independence Day, which is what we used to call the Fourth of July.

Rebecca was legally on her own, but as long as I was paying her tuition, room and board, and automobile insurance I thought I should have something to say about her agenda.

To her, that 18th birthday represented a break from parental authority. She empathized with all those high school coaches who have quit because of parental interference. I told Stan Goldmann that I, at age 52, still felt compelled to please my mother. I didn't want to do anything to disappoint her. I never wanted to, even though I did. "Keep busy," she said, "and you'll stay out of trouble."

Goldmann was tanned and looked terrific at age 63. Retirement and Florida were agreeing with him. My dad was 63 when he died. My mother is 88 and still going strong.

I told Goldmann that my mother had told me when I was a kid that she never wanted to catch me riding on a motorbike or motorcycle. One of my buddies had just gotten one when she offered this warning. And, I can honestly say, I have never been on either.

Recently, one of the Steelers who steers a Harley-Davidson around town invited me to take a ride with him. I was tempted. It might help me appreciate his fascination with being a biker, I reasoned.

"Then I remembered what my mother had told me," I said to Goldmann, "and I turned down the offer. I'd gone along with her desire all this time and I didn't see any point in breaking her rule now. Why spoil a good story I'd often invoked about listening to my mother?"

I don't remember my dad delivering any dictum similar to the one offered by Stan Goldmann's father about the family's reputation. My dad was on the defense a lot in those days because he spent too much time in neighborhood bars. When my mother was reprimanding him from another room in the house, he'd turn to me and wink and say, "I still love her."

So that serves me in good stead when Rebecca is rebelling against her mother and me. We have more rules than any other parents do in the community, she tells us. We're too strict. No one else has the curfews she has, and so forth.

I keep telling her that we're not trying to keep up with the Joneses in that respect, and that we're all wet, but that's the way we want to manage our home and our children. We're doing what we believe is right. We're doing the best we can do. Does any of this sound familiar to you?

Rebecca at eight months in 1978

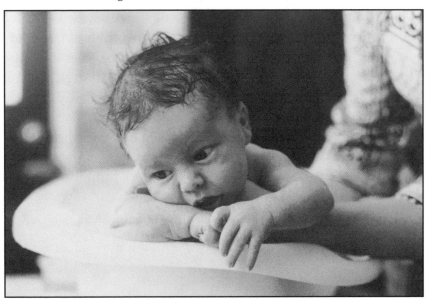

Rebecca's first bath at Long Island home

We just don't want anything bad to happen to her or her older sister, Sarah. It's that simple. We want to help them grow up. Just bear with us. Be patient. You'll be on your own soon enough. You'll raise your own children some day.

Rebecca can't wait to get to Ohio University in Athens this fall. Then she can do whatever she wants to do, she tells us daily. Her life will be her own. It's not easy to be a parent. It's not easy to be a father. I fret over my role and responsibility, as I see it. I worry too much.

I remember my mother's stories about how my dad went out every day during the Depression, when he didn't have a real job, and found work to do, a way to make a few bucks. It serves me in good stead. And when he had a job in later years, my dad always went to work. He prided himself on that.

Rebecca is like that. She has a great work ethic. She gets up at 5 and 6 a.m. on weekend days to go to work. She enjoys the workplace and her co-workers. I admire that. She won a scholarship grant for her all-around efforts.

Some of these thoughts swirled through my mind last Sunday as I sat in a steamy gymnasium for graduation ceremonies at Upper St. Clair High School. Bad weather forced a switch from the stadium to an indoor venue.

Rebecca and her classmates never looked better. I remember how they looked when I saw them in kindergarten and grade school and middle school. Some of the changes were stunning. She looked great, I thought, and I was so proud. She graduated with honors, just edging over the minimum requirement in her final term.

I saw some people in the jammed-in and mostly uncomfortable crowd who were holding babies in their arms. One of the babies, one with lots of dark hair, reminded me of Rebecca when she was an infant.

We'd come a long way together and the best was yet to come. That is my prayer for Father's Day.

Preparing an empty nest
at our home

August 30, 1995

A clock has started ticking in my head. The countdown has begun. Any parent can appreciate our dilemma. Last Sunday, my wife Kathie and I accompanied our older daughter Sarah, as she returned to the University of Virginia for her fourth and final year. How can that possibly be? Soon, too soon, we will be driving our younger daughter, Rebecca, to Ohio University as she begins her college career. Then Kathie and I will become "empty nesters" and things will be different at our home. What will I do now when I wake up in the middle of the night? There will be no rooms to check to see if the girls are safe and snug in their beds.

We moved into our present home in April of 1979. Sarah was 5½ and Rebecca was not quite 2 when we arrived. Sarah will be 22 next month and Rebecca turned 18 this May. They are eager to extend their wings and fly on their own.

It had been a busy summer for Sarah and Rebecca. They kept odd hours. I'd hear them whenever they came home, no matter the hour. I'd hear the key turn in the doorlock. I started to understand and appreciate my mother even more. Now I knew why she worried so much, why she still does.

Sarah worked two jobs for the third straight summer. This time she worked as a student intern in the lab at the Transplantation Institute of the University of Pittsburgh Medical Center. And on weekends, she worked for the third year as sales clerk or sales associate, at Lazarus at South Hills Village.

Her sister was nearby, working as a waitress and a hostess at Eat'n Park Restaurant at the Village. Sometimes she worked two shifts, often the night shift. My father and my father-in-law both worked the night shift when there were more mills and machine shops in the Pittsburgh area. That schedule scrambles the lives of everyone in our house.

She was coming home at 5 and 6 a.m. She'd come home just as Kathie was getting up to go to work, and I was getting ready to start writing. There's no way I can stay in bed when Kathie leaves for work.

Neither of our children shies away from work — outside the home, that is. They inherited that gene from me. They like to work and they like to see their paychecks and, best of all, they can't wait to deposit those checks in their bank accounts.

When they want to go shopping, they prefer to ask their mother or me for some money. I am confident about their futures because they like to work, they are reliable and punctual, they enjoy their co-workers, and they like those paychecks.

Sarah is starting to send out applications to medical schools. She wants to be a doctor someday. She'd like to go to the Pitt Medical School, which would make me very proud. She would live in an apartment somewhere near school, and we could visit her from time to time. Right now, she wants to be a pediatrician. She manages to sneak in some babysitting assignments this summer. She has always enjoyed caring for other people's children. She has enjoyed working at Pitt this past summer, and she knows her way around Oakland and Shadyside.

Rebecca graduated with a 3.56 GPA at Upper St. Clair High School. She worked part-time, about 20 or so hours a week, at Eat'n Park during her junior and senior years. She was awarded a partial scholarship from Eat'n Park as she plans to pursue a degree in food service management.

She has heard they have a mother of all campus parties at Ohio U. on Halloween. We will be passing out candy at our home without any help from Rebecca this year. But we'll be thinking about her, and that infamous Halloween party in

Athens. We felt like the Beverly Hillbillies as we took Sarah back to Charlottesville last Sunday. She drove her own car behind ours, to make sure the mattresses didn't fall off the roof of the station wagon we borrowed from our friends. There were mattresses on our roof, a chest of drawers and chair, and furniture I had to put together when we got there all tucked snugly inside both vehicles. After three years of staying in student dormitories, Sarah is now sharing a house with five of her classmates on the edge of the campus.

She's actually closer to her classrooms than she's been in her first three years at UVA. We'd have preferred that she stayed in the student dormitories. It's a rite of fourth-year students, however, to move off campus, even if it's just a street away from the school.

Our house will be quieter this fall and winter. There will be less laundry, fewer meals to plan for Kathie. She's kinda looking forward to that freedom. She probably wishes I would go away to school for some graduate work. She will miss dogging our daughters' heels, and reminding them to pick up after themselves, to do this or that. I will just miss them and count the days until they come for holiday breaks. Hopefully, God will go with them and look after them.

Grandpap and Grandma Churchman embrace Sarah and Rebecca.

Keeping good company
key to success

August 21, 1996

A huge portrait of Dr. Jonas Salk stood out on the wall in the auditorium at Scaife Hall, which houses the School of Medicine at the University of Pittsburgh. Dr. Salk was the most recognizable of a lineup of portraits of 20 some men and women who had distinguished themselves in Pitt's medical history.

In 1954, while doing research at Pitt, Dr. Salk developed the anti-polio vaccine. It remains one of the most important breakthroughs in medical history.

These portraits lent an impressive aura to the program that welcomed the Class of 2000 to the School of Medicine. Our daughter, Sarah O'Brien, is a member of the class and it was easy to determine that she was, as usual, in good company. Forgive me for feeling more than a hint of pride.

There are 145 students in the Class of 2000, culled from over 5,000 applicants. And 43 percent of them are young women, one of them just 19 years old.

During the "white coat" ceremony, the newcomers donned the white coats, with nameplates identifying them as students in the School of Medicine. They will visit patients and observe doctors treating patients as soon as next month.

Until a few years ago, Pitt's med school students didn't see patients until their third year of study. Now they see them right away, an attempt to get them more patient-oriented in a process called Problem-Based Learning.

This was only the second year that Pitt had a "white coat" ceremony. The students took the Hippocratic oath. They came away feeling like young doctors. Now they have to learn what they need to know to live up to that label. It's a positive, inspirational approach.

Sarah is one of five Upper St. Clair High School graduates among the first-year students, an incredible accomplishment for the USC school. They include Christy O'Neill, Jenny Jackson, Ali Radfar and Todd Blodgett. Kate Williams of Mt. Lebanon, a Phi Beta Kappa student at the University of Virginia, is also in the class.

Miss O'Neill and Miss Jackson have been two of Sarah's closest friends. Miss O'Neill graduated from the University of Richmond with Phi Beta Kappa honors. Sarah did the same at the University of Virginia. They visited each other at their respective cross-state campuses.

Now they are sharing an apartment in Shadyside, just down the block from the main shopping district on Walnut Street. This added to their excitement over entering medical school. Miss Jackson was a dean's list student at Northwestern and is now living on the Pitt campus. Jenny and Sarah have been close friends since middle school. "It's amazing how those girls have remained so close," said "Tommy" Jackson, Jenny's mother, a French teacher at Brashear High School. "They're so diverse. I think that's the source of their strength." Jenny's father, Mel, is a dentist.

Ali Radfar was a Phi Beta Kappa student at Johns Hopkins, and has lived around the corner from our home since we moved to Upper St. Clair in 1979. His parents are both doctors at Mercy Hospital. Ali and Sarah are in the same study group at Pitt.

Blodgett graduated from Pitt two years ago, and has worked and traveled in the interim. "I had to determine if I had the commitment to go to med school," he explained.

There could have been four more students from Upper St. Clair in the Class of 2000 at Pitt. Geoffrey Huey chose Cornell, where he'd gone to undergraduate school. Jim Shanahan is going to Georgetown and Carolyn Pizoli picked Penn State. Kara Pociask was accepted at Pitt, but opted to go to the University of Pennsylvania. Kara has been a close friend of Sarah and Jenny since their grade school days. She

111

graduated with honors in molecular biology from Princeton. (Over 25 students from that 1992 USC class went on to become physicians.)

These kids combined to form quite a think-tank in Upper St. Clair. They studied together. They challenged each other. They continue to maintain a friendly competition.

My mother always told me, "You'll be known by the company you keep." These girls, or young women, are proof of that. Then, too, there is Kara Spaak, who graduated with a degree in English at Notre Dame. She is working with disadvantaged kids in a Jesuit-sponsored program in San Jose, California. Hollee Schwartz graduated from the Medill School of Journalism at Northwestern and is now in Law School at Vanderbilt University. Andrea Hockenberry, a graduate of Michigan, is in Law School at Boston University.

They jokingly called themselves the "Nerd Herd" at USC, but they were all attractive, socially active, diverse, engaging kids who didn't have to make excuses for excelling. They might have been geeks, but they were good kids. They were good for each other. Young students would be wise to seek such company as early as possible. Such students push each other to be the best they can be. You have to dare to be different, dare to be successful, dare to be good kids.

Jenny Jackson, Christy O'Neill and Sarah O'Brien pose after Class of 2000 graduation ceremonies at Carnegie Hall for University of Pittsburgh School of Medicine.

There's no hamster
in our house any Moe

September 18, 1996

A phone call to Dr. Cyril Wecht may be in order. I have a case for the Allegheny County coroner that's as open-and-shut in my mind as the John J. Wilber case. That's what worries me.

If there can be any question about the innocence or motives of the police officer who was dragged through the streets of Pittsburgh by some less-than-stellar citizen, anything is possible. Just ask O.J. Simpson. Then, too, with Dr. Wecht nothing is quite as simple as it seems to be once he starts explaining his forensic findings.

My pet hamster died suddenly this past week in a suspicious manner. His name was Moe. It befitted his size. I had him for 2½ years and now he is no Moe. I believe that my wife, Kathie, killed him in our laundry room. Her accomplices were Mr. Clean and Clorox. It was unintentional, but she's at least guilty of hamslaughter, or Moeslaughter.

Moe was a Russian dwarf hamster. And you thought the cold war was over…

I'd like Dr. Wecht to perform an autopsy. This would put the incorrigible coroner back in the limelight on the local radio and TV talk-show circuit. He should assemble a six-person jury to hear the testimony, better yet six peers of the deceased. That means six Russian dwarf hamsters, with similar markings.

Here's the background story:

This past Saturday I returned home after spending the day at a Prime Sports-sponsored Penguins promotion at the Iceoplex at Southpointe in Canonsburg to be greeted by

Kathie at the door. She threw her hands up, like someone caught robbing a bank, before she spoke.

"I think your hamster is dying," she said, with not a trace of tears in her brown eyes, or a note of grief in her warm voice. "I think he waited for you to get here."

I went upstairs to the bedroom of my daughter, Rebecca, who is away for her sophomore year at Ohio University. Rebecca brought Moe home during her junior year at Upper St. Clair High School for a biology class project. She soon lost interest in Moe and he became my pet. But we kept him in Rebecca's room.

Moe was curled up in a ball and I could tell he was in distress. There was blood around his tiny mouth. But he was still breathing, his belly trembling.

The rest of the glass-enclosed cage was as clean as can be, except for some blood stains on the crushed fill. It was too clean. That's what killed Moe.

My wife, Kathie, is a clean freak. She works as a social worker in the oncology unit at Allegheny General Hospital. She spends a great deal of time on weekends keeping our house clean. She holds our house to the same sterile standards they have for the operating rooms at AGH.

I have come to appreciate a clean house, but I believe that hamsters like something a little crustier and smellier.

Kathie took a whiff of Moe's hamlet a week earlier and decided it was dirty and stinky. She decided to clean it. She placed Moe in a shoe box and took his glass case, or cage, to the laundry room. The plastic house was particularly stinky, she said. So she used some Clorox as well as Mr. Clean on his house.

When I saw the finished result, the hamster's refurbished environment looked too clean. The crushed fill looked like the Sahara Desert after a windstorm. It was in "pristine condition," as Dr. Wecht would say.

The way I see it, or smell it, I don't think Kathie rinsed the glass case well enough. I think some residue or ammonia fumes were still present when Moe was placed back in his abode. It became a death chamber.

He may have done some housekeeping on his own. I suspect he licked the floor of his house, or the sidewalls, and that was the beginning of the end. He died while Kathie and I were at the Pitt-Houston college football game in Oakland. I suspect he took his final twitch at about the same time as the Panthers and Johnny Majors expired in overtime. He was stiff and lying feet up when I found him.

Moe is in hamster heaven now, no doubt. He knows only too well the meaning of the adage, "Cleanliness is next to Godliness."

I will miss Moe. I fed him every day; I'd say something to him once in a while. Writing was less of a lonely business with Moe keeping me company.

Rebecca and her mother and Bailey at Ohio U. to celebrate Kathie's birthday on Halloween.

Moe on my late dwarf hamster

September 25, 1996

I buried my friend and former pet, Moe, a week ago Sunday. He was a Russian dwarf hamster and he fit in the palm of your hand if, that is, you didn't mind him nipping at your fingers.

As pets go, Moe didn't allow you to get too friendly, but I fed him dutifully each day, made comments about him, talked to him a little, and thought we had some things in common — especially when I watched him running furiously and getting nowhere on his wheel. I looked in on him from time to time to see that all was okay.

He was either in a frenzy, making a mad dash here, there and everywhere — the way I work in my office on a chair with wheels — or curled up in a ball doing nothing. That's just like me on the family room couch watching TV.

He had a name, and he was my responsibility. He had belonged to my younger daughter, Rebecca, at first, and then he was mine to care for. Isn't that the way it usually works with pets? I kept him by choice; he was some kind of company when Kathie was off at work, and Rebecca and Sarah were away at school.

I remember the time that Sarah went to pick up Moe and he sank his tiny teeth deep into her hand. She pulled back her hand to shed Moe and he went thataway, smack into a shelf full of books. I picked him up off the floor, a little shaken by his sudden flight, and put him back in his cage.

When the kids were little, and misbehaving in the back seat of the car, I'd holler at them, "Get back in your cage!" That meant they were to split and sit in opposite corners. I still tell them that, just for old time's sake. One of the qualities I liked about Moe is that he let me talk and never interrupted. I surprised myself when I choked up momentarily when I carried him to his final resting-place. I think it reminded me that pets or people we care about could die on us. I chose a small box from The Express that once had a necklace in it as a casket. It had a soft white cotton liner, which seemed suitable. My family has always buried pets with dignity and proper ceremonies.

As a kid, I buried three ducklings named Huey, Dewey and Louie who were wiped out on the same night by some neighborhood vermin. Their burial ground consisted of six Belgian block stones, the sort that once made up so many streets in Pittsburgh. Their burial ground resembled Stonehenge. I still have a photograph of it. I think I hummed "Taps" after I put the final stone in a circular pattern.

I brought a hamster home from biology class at Allderdice High School once and my mother made me keep it out on the porch on a cool evening. That hamster froze to death on our back porch. It was stiffer than a frozen Steakum the next morning.

Mom hadn't forgiven me for bringing a snake home from the woods and letting it loose to scare the bejabbers out of her as it slithered across the kitchen floor as she was cooking one evening. I remember finding a baby mouse in the kitchen cupboard one night that had obviously sampled some rodent killer confection in the cupboard. I put it in a plastic bucket. My mother wouldn't let me keep it, so I had to get rid of it. But I guess I always had a place in my heart for these little guys.

I had my own dog for a few weeks. Its name was Jet, and it was the cutest little jet-black mongrel. A neighbor objected to me having a dog and fed it some hamburger with glass slivers in it. Nice neighborhood, huh? I never had a dog after that. It hurt too much to see Jet die.

Now I'm allergic to some dogs and all cats. The last time I got too close to a cat, feeling sorry for a shabby gray one named La-Mew (as in Mario Lemieux), he sank his claws through my denim jeans into my leg. I lit up like a Christmas tree on the drive home and itched like crazy for a couple of days. I had a similar reaction to being clawed by a cat named Clouseau. You might get the idea that I don't have the best history with pets.

I buried Moe on the side of the house opposite where I once buried Frankie, the turtle, about 15 years ago when Sarah and Rebecca were both toddlers. We'd found Frankie in our backyard and kept him for a few weeks. For Moe, I chose a brand new red brick somebody had given me two years earlier for a grave marker. The brick was the kind that had been used to build an extension on a church and it seemed holier then somehow. Before I closed the box on Moe, I picked a few petals from some pink flowers on my backporch and sprinkled them over him. I also — don't ask me why — put a little shiny buckeye I'd picked up while visiting Rebecca at Ohio U. in with him.

The buckeye will be an eternal reminder to Moe about the Buckeyes of Ohio State who would crush my beloved Pitt football team, 72-to-nothing, within a week of Moe's passing. If Johnny Majors and I have to suffer, why not Moe?

My new young friend next door, John Franyutti, a fifth grader at Boyce Middle School, heard about my hamster dying and felt badly for me. John is a good kid. I've liked him from Day One and now I like him even better because he brought a long-stemmed pink carnation and stuck it alongside the brick as his way of saying goodbye to Moe.

John had been looking forward to looking after Moe for me for a few days when I was away. I think Moe went to hamster heaven. Followers of my column came up to me at South Hills Village and Century III Mall and offered their condolences. They shared some pet stories of their own, warm-hearted stories about their own experiences.

"I'm sorry," one of them said sincerely, "about you losing your friend Moe."

Why we're rooting
for the Dean of basketball

March 26, 1997

A few words of advice for those caught up in March
Madness: Keep an eye on Dean Smith this weekend
when you're watching the Final Four of the NCAA
men's basketball tournament. Coaches, players, parents and
fans can learn a lot from the 66-year-old Smith, the win-
ningest coach in Division I history and man who has twice
won the NCAA title.

See how Smith is usually in his seat and he seldom
shouts at anyone or goes into any tirades. You won't often
find him face-to-face with his players or the referees. He is
usually under control, watching the game. After the game, he
is gracious. He always turns the attention to his players,
praises his opponent and says all the right things. Smith says
that's "the Carolina way."

Smith has always been a class act, and he is a good role
model for all of us. Our family will be rooting for his North
Carolina team this weekend at Indianapolis. Lute Olsen of
Arizona, Rick Pitino of Kentucky and Mike Krzyzewski of
Duke are good men, too, but Smith still stands at the head of
the class.

We have a soft spot in our hearts for Smith because of
the charming manner in which he took our Sarah on a tour of
the Dean E. Smith Activities Center, a 26,000-seat sports
palace on the campus at Chapel Hill named for him.

This was in 1992 when Sarah was a senior at Upper St.
Clair High School. We were visiting campuses to see where
she might want to go to school. We were going to check out
the University of North Carolina on our tour of ACC schools.
I called Smith's office, hoping Sarah, who has been a big bas-

ketball fan, could get a chance to say hello to the coach while we were on the campus. Smith was acquainted with me because I had served as the editor of *Street & Smith's Basketball* magazine for 21 years. Smith also knew I was no longer the editor, merely a contributing writer. I wrote the Big East report, not the ACC report. His secretary called me back five minutes later. She said to stop by.

When we arrived, Smith's secretary came out to greet us in the lobby. She was dressed in a classy manner, like one might expect of a secretary for a Fortune 400 CEO. She greeted Sarah by name. She brought us both a can of soda. She said that Coach Smith had been delayed a few minutes, but would soon be there. When Coach Smith showed, he greeted Sarah enthusiastically. He introduced one of his assistants, Phil Ford, who had been the College Player of the Year at UNC and an NBA performer.

I thought we'd get a hello, a goodbye and we'd be on our way. And that would have been fine, a nice gesture on the part of Dean Smith. "You must be Sarah," he said as he shook hands with my daughter. His familiar squint and smile offered a warm reception. Coach Smith invited us into his office. He asked Sarah a couple of questions about herself and her ambitions. He asked her if she'd had a chance to check out the campus. Sarah expressed some concern about the size of the campus, how big it appeared. Coach Smith showed her an overhead shot of the campus and downsized it for her. "This is where you'll be most of the time," he said. "It's not that big."

He showed Sarah framed photos of former star players at UNC, pointing out players he had recruited from Western Pennsylvania, such as Steve Previs of Bethel Park, George Karl of Penn Hills and Denny Wuycik of Ambridge. After taking her on a tour of the facilities, showing her the locker rooms and training rooms, he took her to courtside where some of the players were shooting baskets. He called one of them from the far end of the court. It was Kevin Salvadori, a handsome 7-footer from Seton-LaSalle High School. He introduced Salvadori to Sarah and they spoke for awhile.

Smith had lost three straight ACC games for the first time in his career — he did it again this year in his first three games and was hanged in effigy on campus — and had a nationally-televised game that same night against Georgia Tech. Yet Coach Smith spent nearly an hour with us and he had Phil Ford meet us after lunch to personally take us on a 45-minute tour of the campus.

Sarah ended up attending rival University of Virginia, which we visited the following day, but North Carolina was her next choice. As we were leaving North Carolina that day, I asked her about her impressions. "Now I know," she said, "why Coach Smith is so successful."

Sarah O'Brien went to University of Virginia and her girlfriend Kara Pociask opted for Princeton University. Now they are both doctors.

Some weeks just seem holier than others do

April 2, 1997

I was scared last week. I was scheduled for a physical exam on Tuesday morning at Allegheny General Hospital, and I was going there with great trepidation. Only two days earlier, I had learned through friends of mine that one of their best friends, a former neighbor of mine, had terminal cancer.

He was told he might expect to live another year at best. It was upsetting. Jim Kosko was a schoolboy sports star at Duquesne High School in the '50s and gained a scholarship to Virginia Tech. We had played tennis a few times in a local league. We both had short tempers.

Jim was my friend Alex Pociask's dear friend. They golfed together and vacationed together. They'd been to Florida in January, during Super Bowl Week, for business and golf. This man has roots similar to mine. We'd both grown up in mill towns along the Monongahela River. He had worked hard, kept his nose clean, gone to college, and moved up the corporate ladder the hard way. His is a success story.

He is 59, only five years my senior. He was planning on retiring at age 61. He was looking forward to more time for golf, his wife and their children and grandchildren. He'd only become a grandfather recently and more are on the way this summer. It's supposed to be an exciting time in one's life, something most of us look forward to in our plans.

Two of his children had become doctors. One of them, a young woman, had babysat a few times for our daughters. The other, a young man, had been our first paperboy when we moved to Upper St. Clair. They were both attractive and personable young people.

It was Holy Week and our daughters were both home for spring break. I had driven to Athens, Ohio, the Friday before to bring Rebecca home from Ohio University, where she is a sophomore, majoring in hotel and restaurant management. Sarah had a week off from her studies at the School of Medicine at the University of Pittsburgh, and was going to come home and be with us all week. I was looking forward to having the girls home again, sleeping in their own beds, being a part of our family for Easter.

I had met that morning before going to Ohio U. with my investment counselor. We went over some numbers in our family retirement program. He showed me numbers that carried out till I was 86 years of age — just four years younger than my mother. If Kathie and I continue to work hard and save for another seven to ten years we should be in decent shape financially for our retirement years. But what kind of shape will we be in physically or spiritually? That's the question.

I have a timeline that shows how old we'll be when Rebecca graduates and runs a resort hotel in the Caribbean, when Sarah completes med school, when she'll be an intern and a resident. Somewhere in there my mother turns 100. The girls should be on their own by the time that we're ready to retire. All so orderly.

Our former neighbor, a corporate executive now living in Cleveland, could look at even better numbers, I'm sure. We played tennis and cards with him. We debated about sports and other sundry subjects with him. He enjoyed a good game and a good argument.

How does he deal with what he has learned about how short his life will be? I remember I thought my dad was old when he died at age 63. Now I think he was much too young. He never got to see our children. They never knew their grandpap on my side of the family.

Their other grandpap was at our home for Easter Sunday. He's 80 now, and just had a year of recovery from a scary physical challenge. After a year's absence, Harvey Churchman Jr. is back bowling and he has signed up for three golf leagues this spring. Bless his spirit.

I had to fast for a day before my exam, and that sent my system into a funk. God forbid I should miss a meal. The nurses, Cathy and Yanessa, were so nice to me, so comforting, and I needed that, I'm almost ashamed to say. I had some concerns that were disturbing. When the doctor told me I was okay, when he said, "There's no cancer; you're clean," I was so relieved.

A nurse gave me a pack of Graham Crackers, and a cup of orange juice and it tasted like banquet fare. I sat on the gurney for a few minutes, so relieved, so grateful, so lucky. I tried to choke back some tears, but I couldn't.

For the record: Jim Kosko was not identified when this story originally appeared.

Alex Pociask with his pal Jim Kosko

Birthday and Mother's Day come early again

May 7, 1997

I can hardly believe that our younger daughter, Rebecca, was born 20 years ago. The date was May 7, 1977, the day before Mother's Day, and her timing couldn't have been better. I was thinking about Rebecca's birthday as my wife, Kathie, and I returned from visiting Rebecca on "Mom's Weekend" at Ohio University this past Sunday evening. Rebecca is a sophomore at the Athens campus.

We kept switching from one oldies' broadcast to another on the car radio as we made the 175-mile trip home. "Does this music make you feel younger?" Kathie inquired.

No, but it sure helped with the reminiscing.

We had taken Rebecca and her boyfriend out to dinner to celebrate her birthday. Kathie had brought Rebecca her gifts and a box stuffed with all sorts of goodies. In turn, Rebecca gave her mother a bouquet of flowers for Mother's Day — one Sunday early.

Rebecca was born at Mercy Hospital in Rockville Centre, New York, about five miles from our home on Long Island. Our older daughter, Sarah, was born there 3½ years earlier.

Kathie had convinced me to take Lamaze classes the second time around so I could be with her when the baby was born, so I could share in the special moment. I could pat Kathie on the back, whisper sweet nothings in her ear, and help her with her breathing exercises to ease the pain. At least that was the idea, or game plan.

I had some misgivings. My history at hospitals was not a good one. I tended to pass out when I got shots or smelled anything that smelled like ether.

I remember the beginning of Rebecca's birth and the end. I missed the middle.

I had felt so confident when I donned the blue gown and cap and slippers to go into the delivery room. I had seen some doctor friends in the hospital hallways that I played tennis with, and waved to them as if we had gone to med school together.

My confidence faltered when the nurse had to jab Kathie's arm three times with a sword-like needle to draw blood. Kathie's veins are always hard to find.

I took a seat at the head of the table where Kathie was positioned to start the birthing process. I was directly behind her head. I held her hand and told her how much I loved her, stuff like that.

Rebecca started to come out "sunny-side up," as they say, or face up when the doctors prefer the babies to be face down as they are delivered.

Our girls didn't believe in coming into this world the easy way. Sarah had been born breech, feet first, and was a bit jaundiced and required an incubator for a spell.

When the doctor saw Rebecca coming out the wrong way, he reached for forceps, and they looked like an iron-bar contraption one might use to crack a 15-pound lobster fresh out of the tank. "I need to turn her head," the doctor calmly explained. He moved the forceps toward Rebecca's little head.

That's when I got woozy. My grip on Kathie's right hand became a near-death grip. I was pulling her backward off the table as I started to sag.

"Nurse," I said. "You'd better get me out of here."

So a little nurse who was a nun unlinked my hand from Kathie's and escorted me to sit in a chair without arms. I didn't think that was safe. I was afraid I would do a "header" onto the marble floor. I had a habit of doing that at hospitals.

So I crawled up on the gurney on which they had brought Kathie to the delivery room. They wheeled me next door into the prep room. "Don't let any of the nurses prep you," the little nun-nurse said in good fun.

I remained on the gurney in the next room for a minute or so to regain my equilibrium. Then I heard a wail. I ran into the delivery room in time to see the doctor hold up a beet-red Rebecca for all to see. I wouldn't have missed it for the world.

Rebecca with Grandma O'Brien in Long Island days

> *"We must always have old memories and young hopes."*
> **— Arsene Houssaye**

Bill Priatko's mother
gave her kids the greatest gift

June 11, 1997

A dear friend of mine was reflecting on Father's Day. When Bill Priatko was 6 years old, he and his brother, John, who was 12, visited their father's grave every day for several years after he died. Their father was 44 when he died. Their mother was 29 when she was widowed, with five children, three boys and two girls. There was no pension, no welfare. Somehow, she managed.

The boys walked a mile from their home in North Braddock to Monongahela Cemetery to keep the burial plot tidy throughout the year, to trim grass and water flowers in the spring and summer, and to say a prayer for their father. They did that for 365 days without missing a day.

"It taught us discipline, responsibility and respect for others," said Priatko, "and we felt the love our mom had for our dad."

Priatko still prays every day for family and friends, kneeling at his bedside to begin each morning. Our family is fortunate enough to be on his prayer list. He is a good husband and a good father, which go hand in hand. He said that Father Hesburgh, the former president of Notre Dame, once said "the greatest gift a father can give his children is to love their mother."

I miss my father more with each passing year. He was 63 and I was 27 when he died. When I reflect on my father, I see him when he was in his 50s, or when he was my age, and he has a smile on his face.

He never knew me since I became a father, and I feel cheated in that respect. He never knew my daughters, Sarah and Rebecca, and both of them missed out on something special. My father was at his best when he was with his grandchildren. He was always good with kids.

My father had his faults. He drank too much and he smoked too much and he wasn't home as much as he could have been. He cared about me and my brothers and sister, but I have had to sort through disappointments to discover that. He was always good to my friends, always eager to feed them something when they came to the house, and was popular at the places he frequented after work, a string of bars between the bank where he cashed his paycheck and our home. Payday was always a mixed blessing at our home.

He died from emphysema. So I don't smoke and I haven't had a drink — hard liquor, that is — in over 15 years. I enjoy a few beers now and then, and a glass of wine with dinner on special occasions. I drink milk, orange juice, iced tea, grape juice and diet soda more often.

My dad was a good worker. One of his bosses at Mesta Machine Company in West Homestead has told me my dad was a dedicated and reliable worker. He was a machinist, a drill-press operator.

A man who worked with him came to me at a shopping mall last Christmas and shared some stories. "I broke in with him as a greenhorn," the man said, "and he taught me a lot. He showed me how to do things, lent me his tools if he thought it would help me do something easier, and gave me good jobs. We were working on a piecemeal basis, but he didn't hog all the good jobs like some guys did. We got paid according to the work items we completed."

You don't hear the expression "greenhorn" much anymore. The man's comments made me feel good. I'd like to think I have those same qualities. I like to mentor young people, and teach them what I know, what I have learned from my elders.

So I've taken on the best of my father, and tip-toed through the minefield of some of the challenges that wounded him. I probably spend too much time in bars, but I enjoy the camaraderie. It's my country club.

I try not to make the same mistakes my dad made. He always loved my mother, and I have no doubts about that.

My mother told me that my father went out every day during The Great Depression. He always came home with some money. He took care of his family. I try to be like my father that way, too. It's a game to me. The bottom line is that my dad did the best he could.

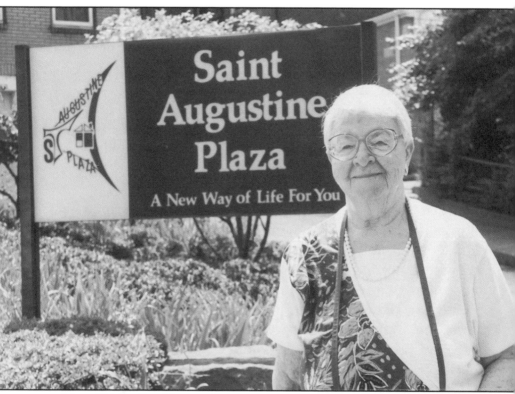

Mary O'Brien lived for nearly 20 years at St. Augustine Plaza in Lawrenceville.

The sweet smell
of a successful marriage

July 16, 1997

A confession is good for the soul, they say. So here goes...I was guilty of deception as well as stupidity in dealing with my wife and a weekly assignment. Every Thursday morning, my wife Kathie kisses me goodbye as she departs our home to go to work and says, "Don't forget to take out the garbage."

And every Thursday I respond, "Leave me a note on the island in the kitchen to remind me."

Every second Thursday is an even more momentous occasion. "Don't forget that today is also the day for recyclables," Kathie adds as she exits. There's a special excitement in the air every other Thursday.

Thursday is also the day that Kathie goes to work one hour earlier than usual. She has to go rounds at 7 a.m. on Thursday in the oncology unit at Allegheny General Hospital. It's the one day that I'm not up and at my word processor in my home office when she leaves the house.

On one recent Thursday, I got wrapped up in my work, writing away. Before I knew it, it was 10 o'clock. I jumped up from my chair in a panic. Oh, no, I had forgotten to take out the garbage. A big black Glad bag was sitting in the garage. What to do, what to do?

Kathie and I will mark our 30th wedding anniversary on August 12. I will be celebrating the event. I'm not sure about Kathie. I have spent much of 30 years trying to stay on her good side, and out of jams.

I didn't want her coming home at the end of a demanding day and asking me, "Why didn't you take out the garbage?"

So I put the garbage bag in the trunk of my car and took off, looking for one of those blue South Hills Disposal sanitation trucks. Alas, I couldn't find any. Then I drove to a near-by strip mall and thought I'd pitch the bag into one of those huge dumpster. But I spotted a sign that warned of penalties and imprisonment for anyone not authorized to use the dumpsters.

I could hear the witness talking to Chief Ron Pardini of the Upper St. Clair Police Department. "Yeah, I recognized the guy. It's that fellow who writes the column in that weekly paper that comes to our home. I'd know that face anywhere!" So I drove off, the garbage bag in the trunk. Before long, I had forgotten about it.

The next day, I was driving with Kathie somewhere, and as soon as we left the house I could smell the garbage. Worse yet, so could Kathie. I cracked the windows to get some fresh air.

"What smells?" she asked.

"What are you talking about?" I asked, incredulously as possible. "I don't smell anything."

"Something smells," Kathie came back. "Did you do something?"

I gave her my best how-could-you-suggest-such-a-thing look, like I've never been guilty of such a trespass. She glanced at a stack of newspapers that I had on the floor between us. "Maybe it's the newspapers," she said. "I've told you not to let those lie around in the car."

"You might be right," I replied, feeling a sense of relief.

We stopped at a service station to refuel. I gathered the newspapers and put them in the trunk. l looked through the rear window to see if Kathie was looking back at me. I didn't think she was looking. So I grabbed the bag of garbage and ran ten yards and threw it like I was doing a hammer throw in a track and field meet, hurling the bag of garbage success-fully into a huge blue dumpster. As a kid, I loved Olympic athletes, and I recalled pictures of Harold Connolly, a strongman from Boston, as a hammer thrower. I had memorized his throwing technique. Such knowledge finally had rich dividends.

I'd rather deal with Chief Pardini than Kathie any day of the week. I was still worried that Kathie had caught me in action. Sherlock Holmes and Jessica Fletcher (of *Murder, She Wrote* fame) had nothing on Kathie when it came to being a super sleuth. If I'm out of step, Kathie knows it, no matter where she might be, better than my drill sergeant in the Army.

When I got back in the car, Kathie said, "It must have been the newspapers."

"I guess so," I said. "As usual, you were right."

We attended a reunion of Kathie's family this past Sunday when I came clean about this story. I told everyone about my sleight-of-hand episode with the garbage bag. Anything for a laugh. No one laughed harder than Kathie. I can still make her laugh. That's why she married me in the first place.

Rebecca O'Brien

Kathie and Jim visit Bailey in Columbus, Ohio

Dancing down the aisle
with a smile again

A famous philosopher, whose name escapes me, said, "Once in a while you have to have the courage to be a fool." Let's change that to "have the courage to be foolish."

Two instances of that in recent weeks come to mind and they both involved my wife Kathie. They were preludes perhaps to our 30th wedding anniversary on August 12.

They were little things, but then again some other philosopher or songwriter told us that little things mean a lot.

On a muggy day when temperatures were in the 90s, Kathie and I completed a series of tennis lessons offered by the Department of Parks and Recreation of Upper St. Clair. After playing tennis for about 25 years, we still think we can get better at it.

We had just come away from the courts. We were sweaty and our tennis outfits were sticking to us. Kathie had to pick up a few items at Foodland. It was a relief to enter Foodland, where it was nearly frigid.

We were in the aisle for dairy products, where it's really nice and cool, when a familiar song came over the p.a. system. It was "That Old Time Rock & Roll" by Bob Seegar and the Silver Bullet Band.

I started slipping and sliding in the aisle, doing a little dancing on my own. What the heck, it was nearly ten o'clock at night and no one else was visible in the aisle.

Kathie was pushing a cart. Suddenly, she stepped away from it and asked, "Do you wanna dance?"

Her inquiry was a song title in itself. There was something about the way she said it — so sweet, so spontaneous— that captured my heart.

So we danced. There was something dangerous about it that enhanced the excitement. What would someone think if they entered the aisle and saw us dancing? At Foodland? In tennis whites? At ten o'clock on a Monday night?

The thought struck me that if we could dance like that in the aisle at Foodland at ten o'clock maybe we could make this marriage work for another 30 years. I hope so.

I have always loved to dance. As a teenager, I used to go to two or three dances a month, mostly at Catholic schools. The girls didn't ask you to dance in those days. Some of them even said "no thanks" after you walked 25 yards across the floor in front of your buddies. The walk back to your buddies was like the Bataan Death March or so we thought when we were 15 or 16 years old.

When you'd get too cozy or danced too close, some nun or chaperone was sure to tap you on the shoulder and caution you to "leave room for the Holy Ghost" between your bodies.

Dancing at Foodland was a warm-up to attending a wedding and reception at Princeton University the following weekend when we danced the night away. I even danced the polka for the first time.

This was at the wedding of Kara Pociask and Colin Nance, who had met during their student days at Princeton. Kara was our Sarah's best friend, and Colin had been a captain and all-Ivy League tight end for the Tigers. He was the perfect son-in-law for my buddy Alex Pociask and his wife Sharon. Alex had been a star center at Michigan Tech.

Alex is Polish. For years, I have watched with envy as others danced the polka. It looked like such great fun. I decided I could do it, dancing with my heart instead of thinking about 1-2-3 steps and such. I think I got away with it.

Kathie comes from Croatian stock on her mother's side of the family, so the polka is in her genes. And she's game.

I also learned never to wear a blue shirt when you're dancing in the summer. When you sweat the stains show.

Late in the evening, I retreated to a room at the hotel and used a hair-dryer to blow-dry my shirt. I was hoping to get back to the dance floor in time for a disco song sung by Donna Summer — "Last Dance" — but I was too late.

I was dry, but the dancing was over. Everyone was exchanging hugs and kisses and good-byes. I was glad I didn't have to scurry around to see if someone wanted a ride home with me. Someone said something funny on our way home to Pittsburgh the next day and Kathie couldn't stop laughing. She just got silly. For me, that was the sound of music.

The Pociask Clan includes, standing left to right, Travis Zielinski, Colin Nance and Alex Pociask and, sitting, Dana Zielinski, Karina and Kara Nance and Sharon Pociask. They have been the best of friends for over 20 years.

First cars aren't supposed to be sensible

January 7, 1998

A New Year began with our daughter Rebecca return-ing to school with the first car that she could call her own. She didn't pay for it, but it's hers just the same. Just ask her. Rebecca returned to Ohio University after a long holiday season in a bright red sports car, a 1994 Mitsubishi Eclipse, an attention-getter for certain. A new fire engine might eclipse it in that respect, but that's about it.

I caved in and bought her the kind of car she wanted and not the kind of car her mother and I thought best for her. Dealing with Rebecca on any issue is akin to root canal surgery and you end up doing anything to stop the pain.

Buying her this first car ranked right up there with teaching her to drive and getting her through her driver's test in Washington, Pa., for degree of difficulty. On top of her post-Christmas shopping list was a two-seat convertible, but Kathie and I held our ground against that purchase. No way, we said in unison. It wasn't practical.

We had a sensible four-door sedan in mind, something nice but modest, something to get her around campus in Athens, something to get her back and forth from home and school in which all her stuff would fit comfortably. That's not what Rebecca had in mind.

"Why don't you do what you did with me?" asked her older sister, Sarah. "Just buy a car and give it to her." We shrugged our collective shoulders. Such tactics simply wouldn't work with Rebecca. It's always been different with her.

Rebecca and I are a lot alike, so have often butted heads. Sarah is her mother's daughter and, while she has her own quirks, she's been easier. I love them both the same. Yes, I do, Rebecca.

I could care less about the cars when it comes down to it. I would prefer they drive military tanks, but my buddy, Bill Baierl, doesn't offer them in his multiple outlets out Wexford way. I just don't want anything bad happening to either of them. I'd chauffeur them around the rest of their lives if I could protect them from harm.

I've agonized over this purchase, worrying that this hot-looking car isn't really in her best interest, isn't the safest vehicle available in America, and I suppose I'll lose more sleep over it before I calm down.

After all, Rebecca will be 21 this May and her track record, in all respects, is pretty good. She's maturing, small signs indicate as much — little notes she left me in the hall-way outside her bedroom during her home stay.

I got to thinking about some of the cars that I had when I was young. My first car cost me, or my mother, about $300. It was a Mercury that resembled a tank, and I think its motor gave out after a few weeks.

My buddies and I used to have to drag our sneakers to stop it on slight grades, I swear. I tried to buy a 1933 Plymouth, an all-black classic with spare tires encased in covers on the front of the running boards. It reminded me of those cars in which Al Capone and his cohorts traveled in *The Untouchables* TV series. Something was wrong with its brakes, too. Plus, my older brother put the battery in back-wards and it discharged rather than charged and I had to take it back to its owner. I'd love to have that car today.

My first new car was a Volkswagen Bug. I traded that in on a Karmann Ghia, a sporty-looking combination of a Volkswagen engine and an Italian body, a two-door sports coupe, anthracite gray with a pearl-white roof, a rare beauty. I'd love to have both of those cars today, too.

When I first met Kathie she was driving an MG midget, a forest green two-seat convertible. Just the kind of car Rebecca was looking for. Sometimes as parents we forget how we felt and thought when we were young. I had fender benders in all those cars in my youth. I haven't had a car accident since, knock on wood.

"It's not easy being a parent," I told my mother the other day.

Mom mulled that one over for a moment and responded, "Tell me about it."

Rebecca shows off her bright red 1994 Mitsubishi Eclipse from Baierl Auto Family.

My heart goes on
as my two girls grow up

April 15, 1998

Alittle girl asked me if I wanted her to tell me a story. She was a precocious child, about four or five years old, with Shirley Temple locks and dimples, and who could say no? Her grandmother, sitting next to her, said she was a chatterbox. She looked and talked like one of those kids you see in a TV commercial, hawking cereal or toys. She started this story about a little girl who goes into the forest, gets lost and finds a kitten.

After she told me the story, I asked her if she liked to read and she said yes. I quizzed her, and she knew all about Clifford the red dog, and Curious George, the mischievous monkey, but didn't know about the little old man who lost his boat but found a new one, a favorite of mine.

She told me about some movies she had seen. Talking to her and thinking about those books and movies, made me realize how much my own girls had grown up, and how much I enjoyed them when they were little girls. I missed those days.

Those of you who have been with me through the years know about Sarah and Rebecca. Sarah is 24, and in the stretch run of her second year at the School of Medicine at the University of Pittsburgh. She is getting married June 27 to a classmate, Matt Zirwas (pronounced Zie-russ). They met during Orientation Week in med school.

As the little girl told me her stories, Sarah was downstairs at the White Orchid in Whitehall, getting fitted for her wedding gown. Later, seeing her standing tall in it, took my breath away for a moment.

Rebecca will be 21 — one of those magic birthdays — on May 7. She is fiercely independent, except when she needs money. This coming-of-age birthday will give her more ammunition in that respect.

Both girls are moving into new quarters this summer. Matt and Sarah have already picked an apartment, without parental approval or inspection from either side, somewhere in Shadyside. Rebecca and some of her sorority sisters are moving out of the Delta Zeta house into a house smack in the center of the campus at Ohio University.

It's a father's dream. It's right across an expanse of lawn from the dorm where Rebecca resided in her freshman year, and it's on a street regularly patrolled by the campus police. Most houses like that are on the fringe of the campus.

The girls are making more decisions on their own these days. They're both doing well with their classes and lives, and finding their own way. Rebecca isn't coming home this summer for the first time in the three years she's been in Athens. She's taking more courses in her hotel and restaurant management major and working as an intern at the Ohio University Inn.

Rebecca didn't come home for Easter, either. Her mother and I visited her and spent the day before Easter with her and her boyfriend. Sarah spent most of the spring break at our home. She spent Saturday at the home of her future in-laws. She'll be dividing holidays with them and us from now on. We have to share her.

Sarah went to church with us on Easter Sunday. We missed having Rebecca with us on such a family day. Kathie had prepared and given both the girls their Easter baskets. They haven't outgrown their love of candy, though both of them count calories more than we did at their age. Sitting next to Sarah at church on Sunday, I found myself checking out the center aisle, making sure there weren't any bumps in the carpeting that might trip her or me when we walk up the aisle together in ten weeks.

I'm getting used to the idea of the girls growing up. It hurts in some ways, especially when I walk into their bedrooms in our home, and see remnants of their days as little girls. "My Heart Goes On," the theme from "Titanic," moves me whenever I hear it, from Celine Dion or Kenny G.

I'm looking forward to the next stages of all our lives. I plan to be a terrific grandpap, perhaps five or six years from now, according to my game plan. The little girl who was telling me stories said she was going with her grandma to church. She told me she was taking her crayons and coloring book. She said goodbye and then waved to me.

Rebecca and Sarah are squeaky clean after bath.

> **"The only thing that's constant in life is change."**
> **— Chuck Noll**

In the pink as family wedding day approaches

June 24, 1998

The sound of my stomach doing flip-flops woke me Monday. It was no way to start such an important week in the life of our family.

"Do you hear that noise?" I asked my wife, Kathie.

"Yes! Is that your stomach?"

Before I retired the night before, I'd eaten homemade apple pie ala mode — and rinsed it down with ice water, and I didn't hear any noises after. So I guess the only explanation for the growling was because I was nervous about the wedding.

Our first-born daughter, Sarah, is marrying Matthew Zirwas this Saturday afternoon. Some people have difficulty saying Matt's last name. "It's Zirwas . . . as in Virus," he says. My first job out of college was as a copy writer for an ad agency. I suggest to my future son-in-law it might not be such a good idea for a doctor to tell people his name rhymes with virus.

He and Sarah have finished their second year of medical school at the University of Pittsburgh. He thinks he wants to be a dermatologist. If I don't stay out of the sun, I might be his first patient — with skin cancer.

I'm in the pink as the big day approaches. I would rather be in the white, which will look better with my black tuxedo. I got sunburned Sunday. Just my face and shins and ankles, mind you, but I hope it will fade soon.

Kathie, Sarah and I went to the Woodland Hills Swim Club Saturday to relax. I wore long shorts and two T-shirts. I took a tube of sun screen lotion and a baseball cap. I wore neither. Instead, I found a tree-shaded spot where I could stretch out and read.

143

John Grisham's *The Rainmaker* was my book choice, as if we haven't had enough rain in our lives this month. It was so dark, so shaded, in this spot I selected that I figured I didn't have to apply the sun screen or wear the baseball cap. I was wrong. When you're a pale-faced Irishman, the sun seeks you out, like a heat-seeking missile, even if you're in a cave, peat bog or a neighborhood bar.

"The Irish were not meant to be out in the sun," New York Giants' owner Wellington Mara once warned me as he squinted into an afternoon sun at Pace University where his team was practicing. My wife and daughter were stretched out in the sun about 25 yards away from me. Neither of them came home with as much color as I did. When will I learn?

This summer is the 100th anniversary of Kennywood Park. It's the 47th anniversary of me getting burned so badly at the old swimming pool at Kennywood Park that I couldn't turn over in my bed that night. My sister, Carole, had abandoned me, an 8-year-old child, in favor of boyfriends that afternoon. I spent the day walking around the rim of the pool searching for her. And I got burnt like you wouldn't believe. Sarah told me over the weekend she wanted me to rent a vest to go with the tuxedo. All the guys in the wedding were wearing vests, she said. Then, too, I think she thought a vest would do a better job of hiding my stomach than a cummerbund.

If my face doesn't get paler between now and the picture-taking session, she may ask me to rent a mask as well. Then I can go to the wedding as the Phantom of the Opera. I was eating the apple pie with my pal, Alex Pociask, on my back porch. I was seeking some last-minute wisdom from a man who'd been there. His daughter, Kara, also a second-year medical student, was married the previous July. His wife, Sharon, was visiting their daughter and her husband, Colin Nance, in Philadelphia over the weekend.

"I went golfing a lot right before the wedding," said Alex. "That's to take your mind off it."

I don't golf. Some of the reasons I don't golf are because I find it frustrating and stressful. Stomach-turning, indeed. Plus, it's another place where I'd surely get sun-burned. I'll be okay. I just want the wedding and reception to be perfect. The reason I am so restless, though, is because I want the marriage to be perfect. That's all. Is that asking too much?

Sarah takes a plane ride at Baldwin, Long Island amusement park.

Lightning, thunder accompany wedding bells

July 1, 1998

A little boy nudged toward me and his name was Noah. Somehow I knew that Noah was going to show up at my daughter's wedding this past Saturday. This was right after the wedding ceremony concluded, and I was standing in a bit of a daze in the parlor of Westminster Presbyterian Church.

Sarah O'Brien was wed to Matthew Zirwas on a magical day that began and ended in a deluge. In between, there was a beautiful union of two young and promising medical school students in a celebration witnessed by family and friends.

Those who were there will never forget the wedding. Organist Bill Evans and cellist Darlene Van Mastright were accompanied in their interlude by percussion from the heavens, roaring thunderclaps and lightning bolts framed in the huge windows of the church.

Mrs. Van Mastright had been Sarah's instructor, teaching her to play the cello in her home in South Park. Tears were streaming down the teacher's face as she played. It was just as stirring when soloist Mary Hughes sang "One Hand, One Heart."

Fierce thunderstorms swamped parts of eight states. It would take our younger daughter, Rebecca, 6½ hours to make what is usually a 3½ hour trip back to Ohio University the next day because of detours caused by flooding. The rain started coming down hard about an hour before the wedding. Many coming to the wedding were drenched getting from their cars to the church.

Rich Carlson of C&R Limousine Service in McMurray had to squeeze a 1998 Lincoln 10-seat stretch limousine into the garage of our home to pick up the women in the bridal party so they wouldn't get wet. Carlson gave up his body and his tuxedo as he stood in the rear of the church, holding a huge umbrella and helping the girls get out of the car to bolt under a too-short entry cover. Carlson was soaking wet and had to go home and exchange his tuxedo for a dark suit.

Seeing Sarah holding her white gown up to her chest, coming out of that limousine like a tailback bolting through the line is a memory I will cherish forever. The bridal party came in a long white limo, but an ark with Noah at the helm might have been more suitable. I never saw it rain so hard. It was like standing directly under Niagara Falls. As it turned out, the stormy weather only heightened the drama. Rev. Robert Norris, who officiated at the ceremony, took the foul weather as a cue to urge the newlyweds to consider the overhead noise as thunderous applause, and the rain drops as confetti celebrating their wedding.

I thought it was a reminder that things don't always go the way we, or in our case, the way my wife, Kathie, plans them. Marriages are certainly like that. It helps to be flexible, patient, faithful, persistent and optimistic.

The reception at the King's Garden of the Pittsburgh Hilton was more like what we had in mind. A wonderful view of Point State Park and the hills surrounding the Three Rivers provided a perfect backdrop for dinner and dancing. When a storm came late in the dark of the night, lightning provided a fireworks show.

Kara Pociask Nance, one of the bridesmaids, offered a moving toast about friendship to Sarah. Sarah's sister, Rebecca, and three of Sarah's friends, Jenny Jackson and Christine O'Neill of Upper St. Clair and Virginia Lao of Washington, D.C., provided attractive pairings with Matt's buddies from Hermitage, Pa.

I was stunned when I saw Kathie in a shimmering white gown, and our daughter Sarah looked much like Kathie did the day I married her nearly 31 years ago. Sekhar Dharmarajan, one of Sarah's classmates at the School of Medicine at the University of Pittsburgh, said that in India it is a good omen when it rains on a wedding day.

Sarah said that, for the rest of her life, whenever she hears thunder or sees lightning, she will be reminded of her wedding day.

Sarah and Matt Zirwas on wedding day on June 27, 1998.

Bailey is next best thing to a grandchild

August 26, 1998

I am going to miss Bailey when she goes back to school next week. Our younger daughter, Rebecca, brought Bailey home with her last Wednesday night when she returned during the summer break. Our home hasn't been the same.

Bailey is an 11-week-old puppy, mostly chow chow, we are told, and who knows what else. I think she has some golden retriever in her, too. I call her a golden chow. Rebecca's friend, Jason Cate, gave Bailey to her as a gift. Jason rescued Bailey from being put to sleep, as they say, at a dog pound in Cleveland.

I think about that every time I see Bailey.

It was a smart move on Jason's part, but one that my wife, Kathie, and I questioned at the time. Rebecca has been begging us for a dog from the day she was born 21 years ago. We still have drawings on display on the wall in our basement Rebecca did in first or second grade expressing her desire to have a dog of her own.

We begged off. Kathie and I both had allergy problems, as did Sarah, our older daughter. Kathie prides herself on keeping a squeaky clean home and dogs leave smells and hair behind them. It never seemed like a good idea.

Having Bailey in our home this past week, however, has been a blessing. She's good company. It has been both a demanding and a relaxing experience. Rebecca and I have taken turns taking Bailey out for her constitutional at about 5:30 to 6 a.m. Rebecca has been working at Eat'n Park during the holiday break and I have been looking after Bailey most of the time.

Before I get caught up with the wonders of having a dog in our home, Kathie has cautioned me that winter will soon be here. It wouldn't be that much fun going out for a walk with Bailey when there's snow on the ground, accompanied by chilling winds.

I will just enjoy her while she is here. Rebecca stayed at Ohio U. this summer to take a class, serve an internship at the Ohio University Inn, and to work at a restaurant to make some spending money. She and some friends have rented a home.

We have missed her. We miss Sarah, who was married in June. Her husband, Matt Zirwas, is the apple of her eye these days. We see them from time to time, but Sarah is not exclusively ours anymore. She is so happy, though. That helps.

I have enjoyed this dog-sitting. "It's like having a baby in the house," said Kathie, and she meant it in the best of ways. There are no diapers to change, or bottles to warm. But Bailey has to do her business every now and then, her water bowl has to be filled regularly and she has to be fed on schedule. And petted. Having my own Grandpuppy feels great.

Rebecca has done a good job of training her. She is well-behaved, playful and obedient, most of the time anyhow. Sometimes she reminds me a lot of Rebecca. She has a mind of her own.

Bailey is also furry, soft and warm. She has attracted all the dog lovers in our development, and I've become more popular.

Our neighbors, the Franyuttis, bought me a copy of *The Encyclopedia of the Dog*, a plateful of colorful milk bones and a toy ball that jingles for Bailey.

We have had more breeds and varieties of dogs pause with their owners at the bottom of our front yard to say hello and hug Bailey; It was like having our own Westminster Kennel Dog Show. Bailey is light brown, with some black markings on her mug and back, and a two-inch strip of silver at the tip of her fluffy and flamboyant tail. She's beautiful.

The real dog lovers hug and kiss her, and say nice things. I have met so many neighbors with Bailey at my side. It reminded me of the days when we took the girls for long walks when they were babies. We would stroll the sidewalks of our Long Island neighborhood, pushing their carriages. It was relaxing, good exercise and a great way to meet everyone in the neighborhood.

Sarah and Matt had Kathie, Rebecca and me over to their Shadyside apartment on Sunday for a birthday cake that Sarah made for me. This is the month when I turned 56 and Kathie and I marked our 31st wedding anniversary.

Rebecca had us watch a cable channel called Animal Planet, which is for pet-lovers. We watched it more when we got home on Sunday. Bailey was so happy to see us.

That is the other great thing. She is always so happy to see us. Yeah, I am going to miss Bailey when school starts.

Bailey, the O'Briens' grandpuppy, relaxes on southern California apartment deck.

Kids at play a picture out of pleasant past

October 28, 1998

A purple football will get your attention, in a hurry. It was one of those Nerf footballs, spongy, light and easy to pitch and catch. Three little kids were playing pass-and-catch and tackling each other.

The three of them were running here and there, and two of them would leap on the back, or grab the legs, of the ball-carrier, and the three of them would tumble into a pile of leaves.

They were laughing, easily, innocently, and the spirited activity and the chill that was in the air flushed their faces.

I was driving by this home in our neighborhood when I spotted the kids playing in the corner lot. I slowed down to watch them. When was the last time you saw kids at play in your neighborhood?

There were plastic pumpkins near the front door of the home. There were scarecrows supported by the lamppost across the street, skeletons and ghosts hanging from nearby trees. It was a pleasant picture, one that would appeal to Norman Rockwell, and the artist who used to draw those wonderful covers for the likes of the *Saturday Evening Post.*

I remembered when I first moved into the neighborhood nineteen years earlier. I got some of the kids into a game of football in my back yard. We just threw the ball up for grabs and tackled whoever had the ball. The kids acted like I had invented a new sport.

I asked one of them what they were playing. "We're playing football," replied Max Daurora. Dumb question.

When I was a kid, we were always playing football in some one else's backyard in the dark. All we needed was a patch of grass, 10 or more yards suited us just fine, and we couldn't understand why the neighbors fussed so much about our football games.

When I was a kid, we played games, boys and girls together, on the street and sidewalks. There are no sidewalks or streetlights in my neighborhood now. There are no kids playing games in the streets.

We played Release-The-Peddler and Buck, Buck, How Many Fingers Up? The latter was concocted, no doubt, by budding chiropractors looking to drum up business. You took a running start and jumped on each other's backs in that game, and landed as hard as you could, kneeing your pals in the kidneys if you could.

We played It-Tag, Kick The Can, Cigarettes, Cards, Airplanes, games that involved eluding one another's tag. You didn't have to go to Toys 'R Us to get any apparatus to play these games. We drew a HopScotch grid in the center of the street with chalk.

When we got a little older, we played Spin-The-Bottle, an excuse to kiss the girls, and you hated it when you ended up matched with one of your cousins.

I was so stunned by seeing kids at honest play, without parents or coaches screaming at them on the sideline, that I stopped to get names.

Patricia Daurora was raking leaves into piles while her two children, Maria and Max, played with a neighbor. Mike Bagdy, Maria and Max are students at St. Thomas More in Bethel Park. Maria is in fifth grade and Max is in third grade. Mike is a third grader at St. Louise DeMarillac.

Watching Patricia raking leaves into piles and then seeing the kids plunge into those piles brought back some good memories. Raking leaves wasn't the chore it is these days when our daughters, Sarah and Rebecca, were taking turns jumping into them.

"It's definitely more fun when you're burying your kids in the leaves," laughed Patricia Daurora.

I thought about a little boy that I had seen in the neighborhood a few weeks earlier, wearing a Johnny Reb Civil War outfit, and how he'd caught my eye for similar reasons. When's the last time you saw a kid playing "war" in your neck of the woods?

Some people think it's a good thing that kids don't play "war" anymore. I'm not so sure. Then, like in a Henry James novel, that same kid in the same uniform appeared before me, marching with a toy rifle over his shoulder in his driveway.

He was by himself, so I didn't stop to ask him his name. He was a lone sentinel. He will have to remain an unknown soldier. I hope to see him again when the kids come to our door for trick-or-treat on Halloween.

Rebecca was wearing her dance recital outfit when she took a ride on backyard swing.

Weekends with Bailey
bring out the best in dog people

January 27, 1999

A neighbor, Edith Johnson, was looking forlorn in her front yard. She told me how she and her husband Bob had to take their dog to the vet to be put to sleep because the dog was old and sick.

The dog was a miniature Yorkshire Terrier named ChitChat. As Edith told me her tale of woe, she must not have been satisfied with my responses. I suppose I wasn't offering much comfort. Suddenly, she looked me in the eyes and said, "You're not a dog person, are you?"

I confessed I was not. I couldn't console her or fathom feeling that passionately about a pet dog. I apologized, but told her I knew someone who was a dog person and would have that person call her.

Martha Babbitt, a friend of my wife Kathie, had a difficult time when her dogs died and sought help to get through her grief. Her minister even called upon her to comfort her. Edith knew Martha, as it turned out. They went to the same church. Martha called Edith to lend her a kind ear.

That was four years ago. The Johnsons have moved to a retirement community in Georgia. When I walk by their former home, taking my daughter's dog, Bailey, for a walk, I think about them. Now I understand. Now I am a dog person, too. The dogs in the neighborhood know it. Now they come up to me, lick my hand and want to be petted. They know I've changed. For years, I never sought out the attention of anyone's dog. Now I pet them all, even the big dogs.

Bailey is eight months old. I mentioned her in this space about six months ago when my younger daughter, Rebecca, first brought her home from Ohio University. Rebecca's boyfriend at the time, Jason Cate, saved Bailey from being put to sleep at a dog shelter in Cleveland, and gave her to Rebecca as a gift.

Rebecca always wanted a dog, but we denied her such a pet for 21 years for one reason or another. Kathie wasn't too thrilled when she heard Rebecca had a dog in the house she shares with three other students at Ohio U. When Rebecca brought Bailey home, however, the dog stole our hearts. We loved her, for starters, because she belonged to Rebecca. She warmed quickly to us. Bailey became our grandpuppy.

Bailey was restricted to the kitchen and laundry room on her initial visits. This past weekend, she had the run of the house, save for the living and dining rooms. She was sleeping at the bottom of our bed. "I've lost complete control," said Kathie with a sigh.

I wish Bailey were lying next to my chair as I write this, but she and Rebecca are back at school. There's a void in our house. I miss Rebecca and her sister, Sarah. I loved it when they were home for the holidays, when Kathie had some days off, and we were all together.

When Bailey is here, she follows me from one room to another. She flops on the floor next to me when I am writing. When I come home, she's excited to see me. She's excited to see everyone. She still has a lot of puppy in her. When we go for walks, she wants to meet, nuzzle and sniff every dog. No matter how big they are or how loud they bark, she wants to get near them.

She wants to meet adults and kids. She's a good neighbor. We could all take a cue from her friendliness. She's mostly Chow Chow, a Chinese-breed unique for their black-purple tongues, with a definite Golden Retriever influence. Dog people are a special breed, I have learned. I've met so many nice people and dogs because of Bailey. They bond with each other.

Our new friends include Sugar and Spice, a pair of English setters, and Rico, Bonnie, Truffles, Spooky, Snowball, Champ, Rudy, Tucker, Hobie, Sonny, Nittany, Buckeye, Beauregard, Lloyd and Molly.

Bailey is an auburn-colored mid-size dog, fluffy and frisky, full of fun. I can't get over how much I love and enjoy this dog. I don't think I would have been as thrilled about taking her for walks when the weather was so bad, but it's been nice weather when she's here.

It's the next best thing to having a grandchild.

Bailey and Rebecca

Delivering first baby
is a special thrill for doctors

February 3, 1999

A message remains on our telephone answering machine that I'm in no hurry to erase. It's from our daughter, Sarah, and it goes like this: "Hi, guys, I just wanted you to know that I helped deliver a baby today! Thought you'd like to know…"

I listened to it more than once, and the excitement and joy in Sarah's voice was unmistakable. Her thrill became her father's thrill. One of my babies was helping to deliver somebody else's baby. Sarah O'Brien is a third-year medical school student at the University of Pittsburgh, doing rotations in every medical specialty at area hospitals. Magee-Womens Hospital is her latest stop.

When I called Sarah to talk to her about assisting in the delivery of a baby (it was a boy), she said she was surprised by how slippery the baby was, and how she had a difficult time holding the baby when he presented himself.

There was a flashback to Sarah's first day in this world when I saw her for the first time and she was in an incubator at Mercy Hospital in Rockville Centre on Long Island. A pediatrician who was our neighbor, Dr. Stuart Eichenfield, assured me that she was just in there as a precaution that she'd be fine and out of there the next day.

I spoke to three physicians and a medical student from the South Hills over the weekend and they all said that delivering that first baby was something they will always remember from their third year of medical school at Pitt.

"Seeing the start of a new life is a thrill," said one of Sarah's classmates, Ali Radfar, who lives just around the corner from our home in Upper St. Clair. Ali and Sarah went to Upper St. Clair High School together.

There are two doctors who play in our weekend basketball games in Upper St. Clair. When asked to name a special thrill from their student days, they quickly mentioned participating in delivering a baby.

"Yeah, you never forget how you felt," said Dr. Bob Flanigan of Peters Township. Dr. Flanigan grew up in West Mifflin and lettered as a lineman for Johnny Majors in 1974. "I didn't want to deliver babies for the rest of my life, but it was a special thrill."

Dr. Flanigan is a gastroenterologist, looking after stomach disorders, at Mercy Hospital. Dr. Mike Bonie is an obstetrician/gynecologist dealing, of course, with women's care at West Penn Hospital. He grew up in Bethel Park, played basketball at Seton-LaSalle, and now lives in Mt. Lebanon.

"I also remember when I was doing a surgery rotation the doctor told me to hold my finger on a major artery of a woman who was bleeding badly from a tear. He told me her life depended on me. That got my attention in a hurry. That's when I got the bug to become a surgeon."

Dr. Richard DiIlio, director of emergency room care at Canonsburg Hospital, said he still remembers how he was caught off guard by how slippery the baby was in his first effort as a medical school student.

"It was like a greased pig," he recalled with a smile. "I ended up grasping it around the ankle. That's something you won't forget. A birthday is always amazing. The third and fourth years of medical school are special, it's a time to learn and to have fun."

Dr. DiIlio said there are times when a baby must be delivered in the emergency room, but it's been at least three years since he last had to do it himself. "It's still a challenge to catch and hold them," he said.

Ali Radfar said he recently had another thrill, observing a procedure at Children's Hospital in which an implant enabled a two-year-old boy to hear for the first time.

"Now he'll be able to hear cars, hear his parents," Radfar remarked. "The doctors were all so happy and excited to do it. That was good to see, too. They've changed the course of that kid's life."

A friend of mine, Gerry Hamilton, said her daughter Jana was an Army nurse in the Labor and Delivery unit of Second General Hospital in Germany in the late '80s. There was only one doctor on duty in that unit and he was busy with another delivery when Jana got a call from Admissions that a woman who was ready to deliver was on her way up on the elevator. When the girl arrived, Jana could see from the bulge in her pantleg that the baby's head had already emerged, so she laid the woman down on the floor and delivered the baby in the hallway. "I remember her calling me," said Gerry Hamilton. "She said, 'Mom, I'm famous. I delivered a baby in the hallway!' You don't forget things like that."

Sarah's first day was spent in incubator "as a precaution," according to her pediatrician, Dr. Stuart Eichenfeld, at Mercy Hospital in Rockville Centre.

Rain is a reminder
of special day in our lives

June 30, 1999

Saturday morning came up hot and dry. A busy but leisurely day was in store. It began with two hours of basketball at the municipal courts in Upper St. Clair, followed by two hours of trimming shrubs in our front yard.

For the record, I scored more points trimming the shrubs than I did playing basketball. It's always been that way. I remembered, for some reason, how I used to please my mother with my precise hedge-trimming skills as a child. So I always drew the assignment each Saturday, because my older brother, Dan, was much more haphazard in his approach to the task.

I think he had read Mark Twain's *Tom Sawyer*, and learned something from the chapter about painting fences, or how to avoid painting fences.

My neighbor, Scott Moore, was watering his lawn as I was trimming the shrubs. "Do you think," he called out, "that we'll ever get any rain?"

I reminded Mr. Moore that it was this same Saturday the year before that we had a deluge, a dramatic downpour that caused flooding in the tri-state area. It began just as we were leaving our home to go to church for the wedding of our daughter, Sarah, and Matt Zirwas.

It was nearly impossible to get into or out of the car to get to the altar that memorable day. We had more rain in 15 minutes that afternoon than we've had in the whole month of June this year. This time we are in a drought. No one was wearing dry clothes when they came into the church for the wedding ceremony.

That Saturday a year ago was June 27, a day later on the calendar.

Last Friday night, my wife, Kathie, and I, along with our younger daughter, Rebecca, met Sarah and Matt for their first anniversary dinner at The Colony Restaurant, where Green Tree says hello to Scott and Mt. Lebanon.

Matt and Sarah still have a honeymoon glow about them. They are happy in their relationship and excited about what they are doing in their lives. Only the week before they had begun their fourth and final year at the School of Medicine at the University of Pittsburgh.

Sarah had spent the week looking after premature babies at Magee Women's Hospital. She had been caring for a baby only the day before that weighed just over one pound. It was born at 26 weeks. Sarah said she had worked the day before from 7 a.m. till 5 p.m. with only 15 minutes for lunch, yet said she hardly noticed the passing of time. She spoke excitedly about some of her experiences during the week.

She loved looking after babies, a critical attribute, I'd think, for someone who wants to be a pediatrician. Matt was involved in a research project. He wants to be a dermatologist. A year from now, on their second anniversary, they will both be bona fide doctors. A dream will be realized, at last. It was nice to be together again to celebrate the occasion. It was less hectic than the year before.

Rebecca is back with us for the summer. She is working at two nearby restaurants, Eat'n Park at South Hills Village, and the Outback Steakhouse, gaining more expertise in her chosen field. She has one more term to go to get her degree in hotel and restaurant management at Ohio University.

A year earlier she looked as beautiful as her sister as the maid of honor in the wedding ceremony. This time around she was working the dinner and evening work shift at Eat'n Park. Sarah spent Saturday afternoon looking after the "preemies" at Magee Womens Hospital. She couldn't have been happier.

162

Kathie and I had two social events on our calendar. We traveled to Irwin to attend a high school graduation for the daughter of one of Kathie's cousins. Kathie's parents were there, as were some of her relatives, and we reminisced about our experiences of that same Saturday a year earlier.

Later in the day, Kathie and I returned to Upper St. Clair to attend a 60th wedding anniversary party for Dave and Sis Shields. They are models for all married folks. Their love and concern for each other is stronger than ever. They, too, were surrounded by family and friends.

It's too bad Sarah and Matt were not there to see the Shields on their special day. Their special relationship offers a goal and a challenge for Sarah and Matt, and most of us married folk. In their case, they have only 59 years to go to match the Shields' streak. It should be fun. On Sunday, June 27, I rushed out of the house and onto our porch when I heard it raining. It was coming down pretty good. At last, it was raining. It was about 2:30 in the afternoon. It seemed fitting that it was raining on the anniversary of our daughter's wedding. This time, I had to smile.

Sarah and Matt celebrate wedding anniversary.

Discovering a former student has become Clemente

T here is a stage show in the city that merits the attention of anyone genuinely interested in the legendary Roberto Clemente. It is called *Clemente, The Measure of a Man*, and it examines the man they called "The Great One," and his Hall of Fame career. It's running for two more weekends at the GRW Theater at Point Park College's Library Center on Wood Street in downtown Pittsburgh.

My wife, Kathie, our daughter, Sarah, and I saw it this past Sunday, and it was a special treat for several reasons. Kathie and I knew Clemente as a young man, and Sarah and I knew Jamaal Holley, who turns in a remarkable performance playing the title role.

We had an opportunity to enjoy a reunion of sorts with two of Clemente's sons, Roberto Jr. and Luis, and one of their father's closest teammates, Manny Sanguillen, still regarded by many as the greatest catcher in Pirates' history.

Sanguillen said he was emotionally moved when he saw Holley on stage, wearing Clemente's No. 21 Pirates uniform. Sarah and I felt the same way, but for a different reason. We had tutored Holley for an hour each week when he was a 13-year-old student at Frick Elementary School near his home in Oakland.

We had volunteered at our church to tutor a middle school student at the Friendship Community Church Learning Center, just two blocks from Pitt Stadium, in 1991-92, Sarah's senior year at Upper St. Clair High School.

Holley was having a hard time with his schoolwork, especially algebra, and we assisted him with his homework on a weekly basis. Algebra was always a toughie for me, as well, and Sarah usually carried the day. Sarah enjoyed the experience so much that she tutored middle school students during her four years at the University of Virginia, and returned to the Friendship Learning Center when she started Medical School at Pitt, just two blocks away.

Now Holley was a 20-year-old sophomore Creative and Performing Arts major at Indiana University of Pennsylvania. And he was up on the stage in a demanding role, mastering a great deal of dialogue, made even more difficult because it was to be delivered with a Latin American accent.

The way he spoke, the way he swung the bat as only Clemente could, his emotional swings, showed that Holley had, indeed, done his homework. Sarah and I shared the pride felt by his mother, who sat a few rows behind us.

I first learned of this show about six months ago when I received a call from Wayne Brinda, the director, who asked me to review the original script submitted by Brian Kral, a playwright from Las Vegas, of all places.

Brinda called me again about a month ago and invited me to attend a rehearsal at the East Liberty Presbyterian Church. When I parked my car on Penn Avenue, I looked to the left and could see the Pennley Park Apartments where Kathie and I resided when we got married in August of 1967.

Several Pirates lived at Pennley Park, which was only a few miles from Forbes Field, and one of them was Roberto Clemente. Yes, Clemente was a neighbor, just two floors above us in the adjoining wing. Moe Becker, the basketball coach at Braddock High School and then Greensburg High School, lived in the same complex.

We'd see Roberto Clemente and his wife, Vera, and their first-born son, Roberto Jr. That's one of the reasons I wrote the book, *Remember Roberto*, back in 1994, when a statue was erected in his honor at Three Rivers Stadium to coincide with the Major League All-Star Game.

When Brinda introduced me to the cast, the kid who was going to play Clemente caught my eye. He looked so familiar. I thought I'd seen him play in some sports contest. It took a while to make the connection to his school days at Frick Elementary School. For him, that was a long time ago. He'd since graduated from Schenley High School, won all sorts of acting awards and scholarships, and had become an accomplished jazz musician. He was a solidly built 6-1 or 6-2, and had grown up quite a bit since we first met. The face and gleaming eyes were the same.

Sarah and her husband, Matt Zirwas, coincidentally enough, have their first apartment in Shadyside, about a mile from our first apartment. Life goes in cycles . . . After attending the rehearsal, I stopped to see Sarah and Matt and mentioned Jamaal Holley. Sarah pulled out a photo album, and opened it to two photos of Holley, showing him with some pro basketball scouts, when we took him to see a basketball game at the Pitt Field House. He had never seen a game there, even though he lived on the next block. One of those scouts, Del Harris, became the head coach of the Los Angeles Lakers soon after. The other scout, Mel Daniels, had been a standout center with the Indiana Pacers.

As Sarah studied the photos of Jamaal Holley, she smiled. "You should ask him," said Sarah, "how he's doing with his algebra."

> *"We never know the love of our parents for us until we become parents."*
> **— Henry Ward Beecher**

Sarah meets her student Jamaal Holley as he plays part of Roberto Clemente

Anniversary cruise
along the city's three rivers

September 1, 1999

August is always a special month for me. Kathie and I celebrated our 32nd wedding anniversary on August 12, and I marked my 57th birthday on August 20. Kathie's mother, Barbara Churchman of White Oak, celebrated her 82nd birthday on August 17, and we shared a cake as we do each year. Kathie baked a chocolate cake for us on a recent Sunday, and I got to blow out the candles — three of them, for some reason.

We added a new event to our August calendar this time around and it made the month even more special.

Nancy Cardiello has been cutting my hair for 20 years, or since we moved here from New York in the summer of 1979. Bill Haines recommended her to me when she was working at Your Father's Mustache in South Hills Village. I have since followed her to the Hair House in Mt. Lebanon, Bellingham's in Scott Township and now in Kirwan Heights.

Nancy not only cuts my hair, but she is my psychiatrist as well. You can't beat that for $20. I can't afford to switch hair stylists; she knows too much about me.

Nancy and her husband, John, who owns his own home remodeling business in Bethel Park, invited Kathie and me to celebrate this cutting edge 20th anniversary by joining them for an evening on their boat. It's a beautiful spick-and-span 33-foot Sea Ray that is maintained at a marina on the Allegheny River near the Strip District. It's called Mr. and Mrs. C, out of Pittsburgh, Pa.

No sooner had we left the dock in the early evening on Friday, Aug. 20, heading northeast up the Allegheny River, than Nancy commanded us, "Turn around. Look at that view! Isn't it something?"

Kathie and I were both impressed by the view, seeing the city's downtown skyline over the waves we were leaving in our wake. We could see the original Heinz plant, which seemed appropriate because I had been telling people that this was "my Heinz birthday."

We went to dinner at Silky's Crow's Nest, a riverside restaurant in Sharpsburg. Nancy surprised me by bringing out a birthday cake she had ordered from a bakery a few days earlier. I was serenaded by strangers who were sitting at nearby tables on a deck overlooking the Allegheny River.

This was the first time that Kathie and I had socialized with Nancy and John, and it went swimmingly well. John considers himself a "considerate boatsman," and we felt comfortable and safe, right from the start.

We could see the best and worst of Pittsburgh traveling its rivers. The potential is so great. There was music and lots of activity at Donzi's and Crewser's and Coconuts along The Strip. When we drove through its streets in our car around midnight they were filled with young people moving from one hot spot to another.

Troll's at Washington's Landing is another popular riverside retreat.

We passed Three Rivers Stadium in the boat around 11 o'clock and saw on the message board that the Pirates had beaten the Diamondbacks, 5-4.

Seeing the stadium lit up at night, looking so good, it's hard to believe it's going to be leveled two years from now. At the same time, envisioning the new stadium and PNC ballpark is an exciting prospect.

Nancy and John are not sports fans. They are boat fans. They spend most weekends on the water, shopping in The Strip, visiting restaurants along the rivers, shopping on the South Side or at Station Square. "I'm at peace here," said John. "It's a different world. I feel calm when I'm on the river, steering our boat about town."

We have been promised another ride on their boat before summer's end, and we asked if we could take the real scenic tour — the one that goes beyond Station Square, and goes up the Monongahela River so I can see the shoreline of Hazelwood and Glenwood and then Homestead. My boyhood home was three blocks away from the Mon. I fished in it once as a youngster — it was an unpleasant experience.

Nancy and I have shared stories and experiences through the years about our two daughters. Her girls are from an earlier marriage. Her younger daughter, Darlene Mauro, lives in Bethel Park, and has two children of her own, Richard and Clayton. Her older daughter, Dana Mauro, is a dancer and actress in New York.

Dana stole the show, *Victor Victoria,* starring Toni Tennille, when it was staged in Pittsburgh last October. Nancy loved telling me about her grandchildren, including three from John's previous marriage, and Dana's latest show roles. We share family photographs from time to time.

It's a shame we waited 20 years to do a night on the town, but we can talk about that the next time I get my hair cut. Kathie has been after me for years to go on a cruise with her, and I hope this counts.

John and Nancy Cardiello are flanked by daughters Dana, at left, and Darlene at Christmas party.

Thankful for those who assist my mother

November 25, 1999

A neighbor of mine was surprised to find me in a different setting. Her bright brown eyes did a roll like a Las Vegas slot machine when she came upon me last week at a gynecologist's office at St. Clair Memorial Hospital. Heidi Hess Boal, the proud mother of six-month-old Elizabeth, grew up in West Mifflin. Her parents, Betty and Darrell Hess, call the baby Betsy. Heidi was in her doctor's office for her regular check-up.

I was sitting in the waiting room, surrounded mostly by pregnant women. "I didn't expect to find you here," said Heidi.

"I didn't expect to be found here," I responded, reaching for another magazine, and blushing just a bit. "This isn't one of my usual hangouts."

In truth, I've been there more than I'd like to admit lately, four times in the last three months. The same office, on alternate days, also serves as a workplace for a team of urologists. Been there with my mother, too. I have accompanied my mother on visits when she needed to see urologists and gynecologists. Having the doctors discuss my mother's plumbing problems with me was not something I envisioned in my youth. Forgive me, but I get a little uncomfortable when a doctor gives me the details of my mother's urinary tract infection in my mother's presence.

The roles have been reversed. Gail Sheehy called them *Passages* in her popular 1974 book, explaining the pattern of adult life crises. My mother, Mary Minnie O'Brien, is 92 years old. If all goes well, she will be 93 on Christmas Eve.

My mother is not sure about that. "I've lived too long," she says, more than once an hour. "I don't want to be a burden to anybody. I pray to God that he takes me. Quickly."

I told my mother it was too late for anyone to take her quickly, even God. Not during the holiday season, I beg. She smiles. I tell my mother that it's merely payback time. That she is getting even with me for all the heartaches and headaches I brought her way when I was a kid. I was the youngest of her four children, born five years apart over a 15-year period. I'm 57 and my oldest brother is 72. My mother is in good hands these days. For the past eight months, she has been living at Asbury Heights. She is in the assisted-living wing of the senior residence complex in a campus-like setting on a hilltop in Mt. Lebanon.

Previous to that, my mother had lived for nearly 22 years at St. Augustine Plaza, a residence for independent seniors in Lawrenceville. I was lucky to get my mother admitted to Asbury Heights when I did. Barbara Kerr, the admissions director, made my mother feel at home from Day One. She often offers hugs and kisses for my mother.

Mrs. Kerr sets the standard for tender loving care, and I am constantly amazed by the way so many of the staff people look after the residents. There is a genuine concern and love. Otherwise, they wouldn't work there.

Mrs. Kerr, by the way, grew up in Homestead and West Mifflin, and now resides in West Mifflin. Her maiden name is Shivetts. Her Uncle Larry Shivetts owned a dry cleaning shop on Main Street in Munhall for many years.

Through the years, I have made speaking appearances at many nursing care and senior resident facilities in the South Hills, and have been impressed by the people who work there. In addition to Asbury Heights, I have been to Friendship Village of South Hills and Country Meadows of South Hills on several occasions, as well as Bethel Park Retirement, Marion Manor in Green Tree, Independence Court and Baptist Homes in Mt. Lebanon.

I've met a lot of good people. God bless 'em. Any of us who have loved ones in their care have much to be thankful for at this time of year. "Everyone is so nice to me here," my mother has told me more than once when we take our walks through the hallways, or in the gardens at Asbury Heights. She boasts about all the activities she attends.

My next-door neighbor, Claudia Franyutti, visited my mother one day, strictly on her own, and played bingo for over an hour. "The people there are so great with one another," she said. "I wish the outside world were like that."

It's difficult at times. Many health issues challenge my mother. She's lived twice as long as her mother. It breaks my heart when she asks me how to spell simple words when she's writing a note to a friend. She's the one who taught me how to spell. She's the one who insisted on good grammar. Now she searches for the right word, and it's out there somewhere in the woods that surround Asbury Heights. It's frustrating, for her, for me. She forgets. She repeats something she said only minutes before.

She is still my mother. She is still my biggest fan. She still says stuff my wife or children will never say. "You work so hard," she'll say. "You deserve some rest." Only your mother is going to tell you that.

One day last spring as she sat among some flower beds, mostly marigolds and impatiens, in a garden setting near a gazebo outside Asbury Heights, she said, "I feel like I'm in heaven." Not yet, Mom. We're still in the waiting room.

Rebecca and Kathie help Grandma O'Brien celebrate her birthday.

Hello, Columbus
and goodbye, Rebecca

December 12, 1999

T he holiday season brings out the sentimentalist in me. I start seeing babies in the shopping malls and they remind me of my daughters when they were infants. I'm carrying them in my arms again, through the streets of New York City, snowflakes sticking to their wool bonnets. They're looking in my eyes like I'm the most important man in their lives.

As I write this, my daughters are both in Ohio. Rebecca has interviews this week with hotel and restaurant chains in Columbus. Sarah and her husband, Matthew, are being interviewed at hospitals in Cleveland for resident doctor positions. They interviewed earlier in Columbus. They had dinner together this past Sunday night.

I was concerned about my children. Sarah and Matt spent Thanksgiving with his family in Johnstown. I never thought Sarah would be spending Thanksgiving in Johnstown, either. My Y2K scare is that more than likely I will not be seeing as much of my children this coming year of 2000.

Have you gone through this? Or is it still ahead of you?

Now I can understand why my mother wasn't as excited as I was when we moved to Miami, and a year later to New York, where we stayed for nine years.

Sarah and Matt are doing residency interviews at hospitals in many cities, and we are as anxious as they are to find out in March where they will be matched. Rebecca plans to begin her career in Columbus, where she has close friends she made during her stay at Ohio University.

Rebecca completed her classes at Ohio U. just before Thanksgiving. It's over. We're so proud of her. She wasn't the scholar that Sarah has been, but she has her own gifts, and she's made the most of them. She enjoyed school in a different way than Sarah. No one had a better time at Ohio U.

She's graduating with a 3.2 GPA and six years experience in the work place, mostly in restaurants, but also in the retail business. She worked 20 hours a week at a book store during her last two years at Ohio U. She also looked after her dog, Bailey, which added to her demanding schedule.

It put a discipline into her life that served her well. Sometime during those last two years Rebecca became a young woman when I wasn't looking. She's matured and tip-toed through a potential minefield to find herself and succeed. As a teenager, she wasn't allowed to hang out at the shopping malls or at all-night restaurants. Instead, she went to work there, made money, earned scholarships, and found something she enjoyed doing.

I was moved and pleased to no end when her mother and I were among the family and friends who received an e-mail thank you letter from Rebecca just before she finished school. I have always preached about the value of thank-you letters. Her letter showed her gifts as a writer as well.

"All of you have touched my life in a very important way," she wrote in part. "You have all been there for the ups and downs of my life and I have been there for yours. I am thankful that all of you are part of my life and I hope you will continue to be. I am a little concerned and worried about this thing they call 'the real world.' Thanks again for all the memories that will all hold a special place in my heart."

Her family is confident Rebecca is ready for the real world.

Father's Day Card Message
"Dad, remember all of the aggravation
I used to cause you? I'm almost done."
— **Love, Rebecca & Bailey**

My mother hasn't forgotten how to say "thank you"

January 11, 2000

I never know who I am going to be when I visit my mother these days. She has told me, on different days, even from one moment to the next, that I am her husband, her "beloved brother-in-law," her grandmother. Then, on her good days, I am just Jim, or Jimmy, her son. Those are my good days, too.

It's confusing and frustrating for both of us. My mother doesn't have much to say to me anymore. She sits in silence and I try to prod her into saying something. She searches for the right words, a reflection, and knows what she wants to say. I can see it in her blue eyes, still bright, and I know it hurts her when her search is fruitless.

"Why do I call you Mom?" I asked her one day.

"Because you're my grandmother," she said.

"C'mon," I beseech her. "Why do I call you Mom?"

She looks at me, a bit puzzled by my inquisition.

It's more than she can handle. Finally, she offers, "Whoever you are, I love you."

I've always known that.

My mother, Mary O'Brien, who lived and worked in Hazelwood much of her adult life, is in residence at Asbury Heights in Mt. Lebanon, just four miles from my home. She has been there about 22 months, the first 17 in the assisted-care unit, and the last five in the nursing center. She went to the nursing center after some bad falls. She didn't want to walk anymore, for fear she'd fall again. She has been in bed or in a wheelchair ever since.

"I like it here," she tells me repeatedly. "They couldn't be nicer to me here. I always try to make the best of it. I'm just getting old and rusty. It makes me feel better when you stop."

The feeling is mutual. Barbara Kerr, the admissions director, kisses my mother whenever she sees her in the hallways. "She's one of my favorites, " says Mrs. Kerr, who lives in Munhall. "She's always so grateful for anything anyone does for her."

The attendants attest to that. "I like your mother," says Dante Ciampaglia, who looks after her in the nursing center. "She's always so pleasant. She never gives anyone a hard time."

When another attendant, Dorothy Tucker, inserted my mother's hearing aids, my mother turned to her and said, "Thank you." She hadn't forgotten her good manners.

"She is so sweet," declared Mrs. Tucker, "and she is so appreciative. We're going to take good care of her. I wish everyone were like her. It would be so wonderful."

Dorothy Tucker asked my mother to identify me. "That's Jim O'Brien, my son," she said, proudly.

"See, she knows," cried Mrs. Tucker. "She fools you now and then."

My mother never complains, which is her greatest virtue. I wish that were in the genes.

I visited my mother on Christmas Eve. It was her 93rd birthday. My wife Kathie came with me and we brought her some birthday and Christmas gifts. I came back the next day. An attendant had dressed her in one of the new jerseys I had picked out for her. It showed some cardinals on a fence in front of a home in a snow-covered field.

My mother's white hair was combed just right. She was sitting up in her wheelchair. She looked nice in her new jersey. She was smiling, and she seemed more lucid than usual. She was making sense. I started to cry. "What's wrong, honey?" she asked. I blamed it on the Christmas season, just getting overwhelmed by it all. She had a concerned look on her face. Once more, for a moment anyhow, she was definitely my mother.

I read her birthday and Christmas cards aloud to her. I recognized the names of relatives and friends, and felt grateful for their kindness. I didn't know some of the names. One of them wrote on the Christmas card, "I think of my lovely friend with the beautiful eyes and smile." Another refers to her "sweet smile." There are people who pay visits to my mother that are strangers to me and angels to my mother. Thank God for such people.

"Whatever happened to me and all that stuff," my mother said when she was feeling bad about her lack of recall. "I'm a complete failure. I forget things I'm supposed to know. I love this place. I just don't love the way I am. Not knowing anything. Jimmy knows I used to be pretty sharp. Don't you, Jim?"

I smiled, appreciative of the recognition. Then my mother had another thought. "I've been so lucky to have the dad I've had." And she looked my way as I was getting ready to go home and said, "I love you, Dad."

"Who's that?" I asked.

"You," she said.

Asbury ambassadors Mary and Jim O'Brien

Walking a high wire
at Dad's Weekend at Ohio U.

January 27, 2000

A squirrel was scurrying across an ice-coated power line overhead, slipping and sliding along the way. I watched, wondering if the squirrel was going to make it. The squirrel looked like it was going to fall a few times, and I wanted to applaud when it successfully crossed the distance and leaped onto the roof of a nearby house. This was in Athens, Ohio on Saturday afternoon.

I felt like that squirrel during Dad's Weekend at Ohio University this past Saturday and Sunday. I attended the festivities with my daughter, Rebecca. It wasn't because the sidewalks were snow-covered and icy that I felt I was treading on treacherous ground or doing a high-wire act.

It was because of my history with Rebecca on Dad's Weekend, and the general nature of our relationship. Sometimes it's difficult to be a dad.

I didn't expect us to be going since she graduated in November, but her boyfriend, Jason Cate of Cleveland, is still in school for another year and she wanted to see him. She sold me on the idea of going with her by telling me his dad, Mike, and his uncle, Phil, would be there.

We all had a great time together on Dad's Weekend a year ago, and I was only too happy to go along for the ride, precarious and full of challenges as that ride might be. I'd had a great time chauffeuring my other daughter, Sarah, to Cincinnati two weeks earlier.

This was kind of a bonus, or a make-up session. I had gone to Ohio U. for Dad's Weekend during Rebecca's freshman year and messed up, I guess, and didn't get invited back again until her senior year.

I blew it the first time out by balking at the idea of bar hopping with Rebecca and her friends. She was under the legal drinking age at the time. Hey, I knew she was drinking with her friends at all the bars on Court Street, just as I drank at Oakland watering holes during my undergraduate days at Pitt, but I didn't want to endorse the idea or be an accomplice to the crime.

Rebecca was really upset with me. I ruined the weekend. She's Irish, too, so it took awhile for her to forgive me. I was so excited when she called and asked me to attend Dad's Weekend when she became a senior. We had both grown up quite a bit in the interim.

This time was different. Many of her old friends were no longer there, of course. When she spotted some close friends, she wanted to spend time with them, no matter the circumstances.

So we ended up Saturday around midnight having a few beers at Zachary's. We sat with Jason and some of their friends at a small table inside one of the bay windows at the front of the bar. We were next to the door.

The door was open much of the time as there was a constant line of dads and daughters and dads and sons standing on the sidewalk outside. There were similar lines in front of all the bars on Court Street on Saturday night.

It was about ten degrees outside, and about eight degrees inside that door. There was a man at the door checking all the student I.D. cards as they came in, or tried to come in. One kid swore at the doorman and the doorman chased him.

I asked the doorman if I swore at him if he'd toss me out as a favor. That was the sort of remark that got me in trouble with Rebecca. At first, she urged me to get into the spirit of things. Then she reprimanded me for talking too loud.

I was doing my best to be cool and not a fool. I was surprised, frankly, by how many fathers were bleary-eyed and walking with difficulty by midnight. Some had turned their baseball caps backward to fit in with the college crowd, but they looked silly to me. They were trying too hard.

I love Rebecca dearly and want to be the best dad in the world for her. Spending time with her on an extended basis, however, is akin to having a date with a landmine. She's the kind of landmine they called "Bouncing Betty" because, when stepped on, they bounced up and exploded in your face or tore out your innards. One misstep or misspoken word and I was dead.

Sitting at that table with the door open at Zachary's was akin to ice fishing. It had all the ambience of a Steelers' tailgate party at Three Rivers Stadium on a similar winter's day. Even Rebecca said her feet were numb.

I was warmed by the fact that Rebecca was at my side, smiling as she spoke with her friends and their fathers. I could see my own breath and Rebecca across the table at the same time. That's what made Dad's Weekend worthwhile and, I think, so much fun.

Photo by Kathleen Churchman O'Brien

Jim O'Brien visits daughter Rebecca and her dog Bailey at home she shared with other students at Ohio University in Athens.

Letting go of children
is always difficult for most parents

March 2, 2000

Most of us parents try to do too much for our kids. We want to help them in all their endeavors, remain involved in their lives and, most of all, to protect them. We want to be their guardians forever. I'm as guilty as anyone in this respect.

Two scenes come to mind from this past week. Twice I came upon mothers and their daughters selling Girl Scout cookies at the post office in Upper St. Clair. Only the mothers were conducting the business transactions. The Girl Scouts were just sitting there, for the most part.

The mothers were counting the change. I find that most kids these days can't add or subtract in their heads. They are lost without calculators or computers. They have to be prompted to say "thank you."

When I made this observation to my daughter, Sarah, she said she remembers selling cookies as a Brownie. "Mom drove me around, but she would drop me off at the bottom of the driveway and I had to go to the door by myself," she said. "I could do math in my head because you guys were always drilling me with those flash cards."

I saw a boy delivering *The Almanac* in our neighborhood. He was sitting in the back of a van driven by his mother, and she drove him from one driveway to another. He hopped out and dropped off the paper. There's a boy nearby who sits in his mother's convertible in the summer, and flings newspapers out of the car as they cruise through the neighborhood. What's he learning from that?

This was one of those glorious days when the temperature was in the 70s. He should be walking through the neighborhood, I thought. His mother meant well, just as I do when I start meddling in my daughters' decision-making.

When I was in grade school, I was good at selling cookies, magazine and newspaper subscriptions, Christmas seals and wrapping paper, whatever we were selling to raise money at school. I always wanted to win those contests, and often did. I went door to door on my own, introducing myself and what I was selling, writing the orders, taking the money and checks, keeping track of everything.

When I was ten years old, I helped my brother, Dan, who was 15, deliver the *Post-Gazette* six mornings a week. We had to rise about an hour and a half earlier than other students in order to complete our rounds and get to school on time. We had as many as 88 customers at one time. Our route covered about a half-mile square.

Rain or snow — it didn't shine at that hour of the day — you had to get the papers delivered. Lightning was a scary proposition. Collecting the money each week was a challenge. Some customers would tell you to come back the next week. Some went a month before they'd pay. You had to be persistent.

You learned how to be responsible for yourself and your business.

We walked about five blocks to school each day, walking with all our friends. My parents didn't have a car when we were growing up.

I'm just as bad as some of these parents, I realize, the way I have been offering my thoughts and suggestions and help with my daughters, and they're not kids anymore. Sarah is 26 and Rebecca will be 23 in May.

Both of them are moving on, in a sense, this month and I am having a difficult time dealing with it. My wife Kathie and I will be helping Rebecca move into her new apartment this Saturday. Sarah and her husband, Matthew Zirwas, will find out in a few weeks where they have been matched to begin their residency as doctors. Even if they stay in Pittsburgh, they will be moving to new quarters.

It's unsettling. Dad doesn't want to let go of his girls. Rebecca is beginning management training at Red Lobster Restaurants in Columbus. She went out a week ago and picked out a one-bedroom apartment in a newly constructed expansion of an existing suburban housing complex.

It looks perfect and the price was right. The location is good and it appears to be in a safe area, fairly convenient to the workplace. I was so pleased and proud of her when we were invited to check out her new accommodations. She is taking her dog, a mixed chow chow named Bailey.

Kathie and I have gotten attached to Bailey, and we will miss her dearly as well.

Rebecca had been working in two different spans over the last nine months at the Outback Steakhouse in Upper St. Clair, where she made a lot of friends. It's not easy for her to say goodbye, but she's looking forward to her new challenge.

Here's a confession: I have to make sure to call Chuck's Auto Service this morning to make an appointment to get her car checked out before she drives to Ohio, just to make sure everything is okay.

Sarah and Matt have enjoyed their four years at the School of Medicine at the University of Pittsburgh. They will graduate in May. We'll help them move, too. I'm not good at moving anymore. I don't deal with change or challenges as well as I once did. I want my girls close to home so we can be a part of their lives, so we can enjoy them.

Good old days: Kathie, Rebecca, Jim and Sarah

No 'Top Dog' certificate appears in store for Bailey

May 18, 2000

It might be easier to get a child into an Ivy League college than to get a dog into a pet-grooming salon in the South Hills.

That's been our experience anyway. My wife, Kathie, and I spent a week trying to get a grooming appointment for Bailey, the mostly chow chow dog who belongs to our younger daughter, Rebecca.

I agreed to have her groomed during her two-week vacation stay at our home this month. Rebecca asked me to do it during her birthday celebration in Columbus, where she is now living, and caught me at a weak moment. Rebecca turned 23 earlier this month. Bailey will celebrate her 2nd birthday this Friday.

We had been happy with our two previous experiences at Nanette's Pet Boutique in Scott Township, but they had lost the groomer who handles bigger dogs and they wouldn't take Bailey this time.

One of my neighbors, Susan Smith, said she had the same response when she called Nanette's to get a "summer cut" for her golden retriever, Buckeye. "Besides, we don't believe in summer cuts," someone at Nanette's told her. "Dogs have their own cooling system."

Some of the people Kathie and I spoke to at area grooming salons seem to be quite direct in their remarks. They asked more questions than Regis Philbin when we would call to make an appointment. It must be what it would be like to face a membership committee at one of the area country clubs.

"If she misbehaves she won't be allowed to come back," someone at Nanette's told us before our first visit. Apparently, Bailey passed her test, though they did brand her as "a bit feisty."

Some of the salons would be happier, it seems, if Bailey had a degree from the Academy of Canine Etiquette & Grooming out in Imperial.

I love some of the names of the places. There's Wizard of Paws in Bethel Park, DeLuca's Canine Country Club in McMurray, Fancy Paws in Finleyville, Furry Friends in Bridgeville, Max's Bath House in Library, Meows and Growls in Venetia, Rivendeel Kennel as well as Style & Comfort in Canonsburg, Amy's Groom Room in Greentree and Doggywood in Reserve.

When anyone asked about Bailey's breeding, we would say she was mostly chow chow or chow mixed, and possibly golden retriever. There'd be a pause at the other end of the phone. "A chow, huh?" someone would say. "Well, we're not taking new dogs right now."

Chow chows, it seems, have a bad rap for being ornery, even nasty, and not comfortable with strangers. This is not true of Bailey, however. Whatever else she has in her blood-lines has given her a delightful and pleasant personality. She warms quickly to anyone who will pet her or offer her a treat.

We were flat out rejected at several grooming salons. We didn't tell Bailey for fear it might have long-lasting emotional effects. Another of my dog-loving neighbors, Lynn Rubin, recommended The Top Dog Pet Salon in McMurray. That's where she took her cocker spaniel, Sonny.

She really liked Dan Giles, who owned and operated the grooming shop on East McMurray Road, just off Rt. 19 near Donaldson's Crossroads. "He breeds and shows dogs and is just so good with them," allowed Lynn. "He used to be at the Bourse Shops in Scott, but moved a few months ago to McMurray."

When I spoke to Dan on the telephone, he didn't grill me about Bailey's background, or whether or not she had pedigree papers. "We'll be happy to see her," he said, "and I'm sure we can take good care of her. You'll be happy here."

Bailey and I both had our hair cut last Friday. I wanted to look good for a family wedding and reception the next day. I didn't have as much difficulty getting my appointment at Bellingham's in Bridgeville. Nancy Cardiello has been cutting my hair for 21 years since I moved here from New York. She took me in even though I didn't have pedigree papers, either. She'd probably say I was a bit feisty, too. My haircut cost $18 and Bailey's was $36, but Bailey had her nails cut and her ears, etc., cleaned.

Dan Giles was pleased to present Bailey when I arrived at his place. Bailey looked beautiful. Her burnt orange hair was cut just right. She didn't seem anxious for her experience. As far as I was concerned, Bailey looked good enough to be shown in competition. But there are no classifications for mostly chow chow or mixed chow at the Westminster Dog Show. That's their loss, not Bailey's. Photo by Kathleen Churchman O'Brien

Jim and his beloved Bailey relax on backporch.

Having a daughter become a doctor

May 25, 2000

Where do thirty young medical school students go to toast the completion of four years of hard work at the University of Pittsburgh? They go to Chiodo's, of course. My daughter, Sarah, graduated from Pitt's School of Medicine at ceremonies this past Monday at Carnegie Hall in Oakland. So did her husband, Matthew Zirwas. In fact, he graduated first in the class. So you can imagine how proud I am feeling right now about the new doctors in our family.

Sarah has served as the editor of the Medical School yearbook and she asked me to take some photographs of events of this past week to help her complete her task. So I went to a dress rehearsal of a musical show the class put on at Carlow College, a spoof on everyone associated with their four years of study in the School of Medicine. Everyone was fair game.

That was last Thursday night. They were finished around 11 p.m. That's when my son-in-law, Matthew, asked me if I wanted to join him and some of his buddies for a few drinks afterward. "We're going to Chiodo's in Homestead," he told me. "Do you know where that is?"

I told him I did. I told him I was a long-time friend of the owner, Joe Chiodo, and always stopped at his restaurant-bar at the end of the Homestead High-Level Bridge whenever I was in the area. I'd been there two weeks earlier.

Joe always makes such a fuss over my friends and they love the guy.

I arrived at Chiodo's about ten minutes before everybody else. I was traveling through familiar territory. I had attended some of the events that mark the end of a demanding four-year trip for these medical students, and they were held in some swanky clubs like the 20th Century Club, a citadel for high society women, and Antonian Hall at Carlow College, and the Commons Room of the Cathedral of Learning. Chiodo's is seldom mentioned in the same sentence.

And where did these medical school students want to go to let their hair down, to empty a few pitchers of draft beer, and to say goodbye perhaps to some friends they had made over the last four years? To Chiodo's, of course.

A lot of college kids go to Chiodo's. They like the atmosphere, all the sports memorabilia, all the colorful bras hanging from the rafters along with football helmets and hockey sticks, all the local characters. They like the way they're treated.

"I met the owner once," boasted a young man named Rob Denshaw. "He's a real little guy. He's so friendly. He talked to all of us, told us some good stories, and really made us feel at home."

I was wishing Joe Chiodo was there, to meet my son-in-law and his friends. Chiodo's is best when Joe is there. But it was past his bedtime. If Joe had been there he'd have surely opened the kitchen so these kids could have some hamburgers, fish sandwiches and French fries. And fun. Imagine closing a kitchen when you have 30 young men who haven't had time to eat dinner earlier in the evening.

The med school students at Chiodo's were all guys. There are just as many girls as guys in the graduating class of 2000. The same holds true for the Law School at Pitt. These are different times. I figured my daughter was at home in her apartment, sleeping the good sleep. I thought a lot about Sarah this past week.

I was concerned about her wellbeing the first time I ever laid eyes on Sarah O'Brien. It was about an hour after her birth, on Sept. 20, 1973, and she was asleep in an incubator in the maternity ward of Mercy Hospital in Rockville Centre, New York. Why was she in an incubator?

190

Dr. Stuart Eichenfield, her pediatrician, came up to me and congratulated me on the birth of my first child. Dr. Eichenfield was a friend and neighbor, living just four doors from me in nearby Baldwin, on the south shore of Long Island. Dr. Eichenfield put his hand on my shoulder as we stood over Sarah's silent form. "She's fine," he offered to comfort me. "She's in here overnight as a precaution. She's got a touch of jaundice." His words and his comforting gesture eased my concerns. I could still see his wavy fox-red hair and goatee as I thought about him and Sarah this past week.

Then there was the time when my second daughter, Rebecca, was having respiratory problems, coughing harshly and breathing with difficulty from a bout with the croup. She started turning blue in her crib. I picked her up, and my wife, Kathie, and I rushed her to Mercy Hospital. Dr. Eichenfield explained the problem, and told me what to do if that should ever happen again. I was worried that we were going to lose Rebecca that night.

It's important to have people who know how to care for us and for our children. That's why Kathie and I are so excited and so proud that Sarah is now a doctor. She will be a pediatrician. She will begin her residency in pediatrics at Children's Hospital here in Pittsburgh in another month.

Sarah and her husband, Matthew Zirwas, participated in graduation ceremonies on Monday for the 2000 Class of the School of Medicine of the University of Pittsburgh. Matthew will be a resident at UPMC. He wants to be a dermatologist. So we have two doctors in our family now. It feels good to begin a sentence by saying, "My daughter, the doctor…"

Two of Sarah's best friends from the 1992 Class of Upper St. Clair High School are now doctors, too. Jennifer Jackson and Christy O'Neill also graduated. Jennifer will be a resident in obstetrics/gynecology at Northwestern University Hospital in suburban Chicago. Christy will be at Children's Hospital here in Pittsburgh.

Kara Pociask, from that 1992 USC class, graduated Sunday from the University of Pennsylvania School of Medicine. She will do her residency in internal medicine at the University of Chicago Hospital. Those four young women have been close friends since their middle-school days, and pushed each other to excellence.

Sarah and her friends participated in a stage show on Friday and Saturday nights at Carlow College. It was a musical comedy about their four years of Med School. Everybody and anybody associated with that experience was fair game. They sang and danced and acted in a delightful parody of their days at Pitt. In addition, Sarah got to play the cello in the orchestra. She's always been so happy when she was in a show with her friends. Baldo Iorio of Heidelberg was so happy to attend an awards ceremony for the Med School at the Century Club in Oakland last Friday. His grandson, Matthew Zirwas, the son of his daughter Shirley and her husband, Tom, received an award as the No. 1 graduate in the Class of 2000. That's my son-in-law.

Dr. Sarah O'Brien Zirwas and Dr. Christy O'Neill Yost served their residency in pediatrics at Children's Hospital of Pittsburgh.

Mom simply doesn't remember as much anymore

August 9, 2000

I took my mother to St. Clair Hospital last week to have her brain x-rayed. The doctor who looks after her at Asbury Heights in Mt. Lebanon wanted to see what was going on up there. He thought there might be some bleeding in her brain. That might help explain her declining mental abilities.

I'm not the doctor in our family, but I felt I knew what was wrong. She's just getting old. She is 93 years old and, God willing as they say, she will be 94 come Christmas Eve. Mom knows, too. "I'm just living too long," she says repeatedly. "I never expected to live this long."

She knows she's slipping. She knows things she can't say anymore. She's in relative good health. There are pills to quell most of her problems, and the nurses and attendants at Asbury Heights monitor her medicines and make sure she takes what she's supposed to take at appointed times.

She gets the best care. I can't believe how patient, prompt, attentive and, in most cases, how loving the people are who look after her. She gets a lot of TLC. She still has a good appetite and never misses a meal.

She hasn't been playing bingo lately, and that concerns me. She always loved to play bingo. "It just doesn't do anything for me anymore," she explains.

"I pray that God will take me," she says. "I've lived long enough. I've had a good life. But I'm tired, and I just feel like I'm a burden to a lot of people."

When I took her to St. Clair Hospital, the technician in the x-ray department asked her some questions to see if she was competent to okay the procedure, which involved minor risk. He asked if she knew where she was. She didn't know. He asked her if she knew what day of the week it was. She didn't know. He asked her if she knew what month it was. She didn't know. Finally, he asked her if she knew who the president of the United States was. Again, she didn't know. So I signed to permit the procedure.

On the way back to Asbury Heights, I asked her some more questions, even though they tell you that you shouldn't do that. I asked her if FDR was the president. She said he wasn't. I asked her if RFK or JFK was the president. She said no. I mentioned Jimmy Carter, Gerald Ford, Ronald Reagan, and she said none of them was the president, either.

Maybe she's smarter than I realize. Maybe she just wiped Bill Clinton out of her memory bank because she doesn't want to accept that he's our president. Then, too, I realized that Ronald Reagan might fail the same memory test. I was more concerned that she didn't know what month it was. I reminded her that it was August, and that there were two important dates this month that she should remember. My wife Kathie and I will celebrate our 33rd wedding anniversary on Aug. 12. My 58th birthday will be on Aug. 20.

I am one of the few people my mother knows by name anymore. She's always telling me how much she has always loved me. She thanks me for looking after her, and taking her places. She's happy to see me, sad to see me go. She still has the sweetest smile. We're still able to talk, when her hearing aids are set properly. My mother used to call me at 3:26 a.m. on Aug. 20 to wish me a happy birthday. It was her little joke. "That's when you were born," she'd say. "You kept me awake that day so I figured I'd get you up now." I'd smile and go back to sleep. That's when I could wake up in the middle of the night and get back to sleep.

I was sitting on the porch the other night in the midst of that heavy rainfall. I can't remember a weekend when it rained so much, or when there was more thunder and lighting. But, as a kid, I liked to sit on the porch with my mother when it was raining. We had aluminum awnings and we liked the sound of rain falling on those awnings. We were safe sitting there together on the glider.

As I sat out there on Sunday night I thought about my mother and how she was faring. I thought about friends and neighbors, who have friends and children who are being threatened by health challenges. I thought about the young golfer in Peters Township who lost his life in an auto accident. I thought about other kids in the area who have lost their lives in similar mishaps.

I thought about young mothers in the neighborhood, at least four come to mind, who've died this past year. I thought about a boyhood pal who just died. Who decides when it's time for anyone to die? So often it doesn't make much sense. It's one of those things none of us understand.

I don't want my mother to die, but I don't want to go over to Asbury Heights some day and discover that she doesn't know me anymore.

Grandma O'Brien came to visit Sarah and Kathie
often during our Long Island days.

A patriot in Ligonier likes to open home for visitors

August 17, 2000

A woman who reads my column faithfully gave my wife Kathie and me the best wedding anniversary present ever. She let us stay in her getaway home in downtown Ligonier overnight while she returned to her other home in Finleyville.

We went to Ligonier on Saturday morning, August 12, 2000, with our good friends, Sharon and Alex Pociask of Upper St. Clair. They had celebrated their 31st wedding anniversary on Wednesday and Kathie and I were marking our 33rd wedding anniversary that Saturday.

Doris Matthews invited us to stay in her delightful home. It's a picturesque two-story gray frame house a few blocks away from the town square in Ligonier, the one with the white gazebo in the middle of a patch of green. The locals refer to it as "The Diamond." It is in the Laurel Highlands of Westmoreland County, about 60 miles east of Pittsburgh.

The Mellons and Scaifes have estates nearby. Doris Matthews has a storybook two-bedroom home in a storybook community, where the pace is slower and kinder. Every room in her home is like a gift shop.

There is an eclectic mix of furniture: antique, country and early American. "There's lots of red, white and blue," declared Doris proudly. "I'm a patriotic American all the way. You'll see our flag and Uncle Sam everywhere."

Each room is full of knick-knacks on shelves, miniature cars, buses and trucks and all sorts of interesting doodads. Everything is so pin neat. There was a guest book to sign. "I love to share my place with others," said Doris.

She and her husband bought the place in 1992 as a retirement getaway, but he died before he had a chance to enjoy it. Doris likes others to enjoy it now.

She bought some gourmet coffee and wine for us, but we had brought our own essentials, food and towels and such. Doris showed us where everything was, recommended places for us to go, and went her merry way.

"Thank God for people like Doris Matthews," said Kathie. "She's so trusting and so generous."

We had first met Doris in June at a concert in the town square. Our older daughter, Dr. Sarah O'Brien-Zirwas, fresh out of Pitt's Medical School, was playing the cello with the North Pittsburgh Philharmonic Orchestra in a Sunday series that continues through the summer in Ligonier. Doris Matthews came to me after the concert and introduced herself.

She said she was from Finleyville, actually Jefferson Boro, and a regular reader of my newspaper column. She said we should come back to Ligonier sometime and that we could stay at her home. Kathie liked the idea of coming back to Ligonier and having the time to take in the whole scene, to visit all the neat-looking shops on East Main and West Main.

She thought it would be a great place to share our anniversaries with the Pociasks. It was an idyllic day in an idyllic town from the past. I like Ligonier because the Ligonier Valley Public Library has 11 of my 12 books in my "Pittsburgh Proud" sports series in its collection. That's a real kick to see that. They have a Ligonier Valley Writers Association, too, and I had been the featured speaker at a winter "hot dog" party the previous year.

Ligonier is a great place for a getaway day or an overnight stay, or to live as we learned from a lot of the local citizens, all Chamber of Commerce types. Doris gave us lots of ideas of things to do and places to visit.

We went to the Country Market at Ligonier, where homegrown produce and down-home foods and crafts are offered from 7 a.m. till noon each Saturday through September 23. Fort Ligonier Days are in October. That and the fall foliage are good reasons to visit Ligonier at that time of year.

We had brunch at The Ligonier Tavern where the menu was as eclectic and interesting as Doris' home. I had a Greek dish, eggplant moussaka.

We just missed former Pitt chancellor Wesley W. Posvar when we arrived and, we learned on a later stop at the bar at The Ligonier Tavern, that we missed WPXI-TV sportscaster Sam Nover when we left. He'd been there for lunch.

I thought we were far from home, but I couldn't get over how many people we bumped into that we knew from Pittsburgh. Then, too, I was wearing a Pitt ballcap and a "Team Pittsburgh" golf shirt.

Alex and I went to visit Dick Groat, the National League MVP for the Pirates during the 1960 World Series championship season, at his Champion Lakes Golf Club seven miles away while the girls went shopping on Main Street.

Groat was a great host, as always, and showed us his Bed & Breakfast establishment where all the rooms are named after former teammates on the 1960 Bucs and have appropriate framed photos in each of them from those glorious days. Groat, too, has been to the Thompson Club sports dinner on several occasions.

We had homemade ice cream at Abigail's Coffeehouse and we witnessed a Scottish-style wedding. The men were in kilts and they marched to the gazebo in the town square to the music of a bagpipe. It rained lightly during the ceremony, not enough to spoil it. What's a Scottish wedding without some rain? We joined our wives for a drink at Joe's Bar, where the owner is a big-game hunter and taxidermist and has all his kills in a display area that fills two stories in the back of the bar. There's even an elephant and a giraffe on display. My wife Kathie was so fascinated by the wildlife display that it made me nervous.

We had dinner at the Colonial Inn down the road on Route 30. It had been years since I had dined there and it brought back great memories. We sipped white wine under the metal awnings in the rear of Doris' home in a light rainfall. "It doesn't get any better than this," announced Alex. As Kathie and I crawled into bed at 10:10 p.m. she said, "This is a better set-up than we had for our honeymoon." That showed that we were growing up as well as growing old. We decided we had to return to Ligonier in October to see the fall foliage.

Doris Matthews opens her Ligonier home to us

It won't be snowing in May in my backyard anymore

November 2, 2000

A cottonwood tree was in our backyard when we bought our home in the South Hills 21 years ago. It was a tall stately tree at one end of the yard, close to the border of three of our neighbors' yards. It was beautiful most of the year. The poet Joyce Kilmer never saw this tree, but it rated a remembrance. It was called a cottonwood because each summer it would turn white, sprouting cotton-like stuff or seedlings on its branches.

That white stuff would soon start blowing in the wind and falling to the ground below, most of it flying into my neighbors' yards. None of them was happy about that. They didn't appreciate this phenomenon of nature.

When they expressed their displeasure or unhappiness, I would tell them that the tree was there before any of us moved in and that it was God's creation. There were meant to be cottonwood trees on the landscape, as part of the greater scheme of things. I knew these people took great pride in being Christians, so I was appealing to their innermost goodness.

It was nature at work. The squirrels seemed to like it just fine, and so did the cardinals, blue jays, woodpeckers, mourning doves, hummingbirds, ravens, finches and martins I'd see on or near its branches. The deer and rabbits seemed to like doing their business beneath it. The moles liked it, too.

Our nearest neighbors, Scott and Nancy Moore, didn't like the tree because the cottonlike substance coated the grass and shrubs in their yard, and made a mess around their children's swing set. I could appreciate their complaint. There were times when that cottonwood tree was just a dirty tree.

The Moores have been good neighbors and I did not want to annoy them. I told the Moores that their children, Lisa, 7½, and Robbie, 5, would always remember that when they were children they lived in a home and played in a yard where it always snowed in May. And sometimes in June. They would never forget that.

We used to have a swing set near that cottonwood tree, too. Our daughters, Sarah and Rebecca, used to ride those swings when they were little like Lisa and Robbie. I remember how difficult it was for me to dismantle and remove that swing set when our girls got too big to use it anymore. I had flashbacks to when my father-in-law and I picked it up and brought it home the first time.

I remember how Sarah and Rebecca used to join me in the backyard when I was raking the leaves that fell from that cottonwood tree. Whenever I'd gather a pile of leaves the girls loved to run and jump in the pile of leaves, and lose themselves in the leaves.

When I would stuff those leaves into large bags they would jump on top of the bag to help me press those leaves deeper into the bag, to compact those piles of leaves. They laughed so much when they did that. It was wonderful to hear them laugh like that, to see the smiles on their young faces. To hear them shriek with delight. Sometimes I can still hear them.

In recent years, whenever I would look out from the kitchen window, or from the porch, I would see that cottonwood tree and it would remind me of those times when the girls would play there and run and jump in the leaves.

I could still see Rebecca running around that tree, getting ready for a skill test in physical education class, or getting in shape for soccer. She used to duck under this one low-hanging branch. I cut it away so she wouldn't have to duck, so she wouldn't run into it again.

The cottonwood tree got older, and it started shedding more and more of that cotton-like substance. It also started shedding its leaves sooner, and over a longer period of time. Now it was becoming a nuisance to me, too. The yard was messier from its droppings more often than not. I started to agree with my neighbors that it was more of a nuisance than a landmark.

I decided to have it cut down. I had about a half dozen estimates on what it would cost to have it cut down and removed from my property. Arbor Tree Specialist had the lowest bid, and was recommended by my neighbor Woody Wolf. I figured a fellow named Woody knew something about trees. I waffled on my decision, changing my mind each day. When the men from Arbor Tree arrived to do the dirty deed they could sense my uneasiness and told me I had one last chance to change my mind. They did an efficient and clean job. The tree is gone. I'll miss it. The yard looks bigger now, like my daughters' bedrooms now that they're gone, too. I hope I can still picture the girls at play even with that cottonwood tree missing from our backyard.

Rebecca and Sarah practice for PennDOT work.

It took a long time before it was finally Father's Day

June 21, 2001

I was sitting on the edge of the bed, taking my socks off, when the telephone rang. My wife, Kathie, answered it downstairs. She called out to me to pick up the phone. "It's Rebecca," cried Kathie. My heart quickened. It was 10:45 p.m. I had dozed off watching "The Practice" on TV and decided I had better go to bed. It had been a long day.

"Hi, Dad," Rebecca began, sounding like a little girl. "Happy Father's Day! I didn't want you to think I had forgotten. I've just been busy working all day at the restaurant. I'm still here, but we're ready to go home now. You'll be getting something from me in the mail in the next few days. I've just been so busy here. Better late than never, right?"

Rebecca has used that line before. I'm used to it by now. I told Rebecca I loved her before I turned the phone back to Kathie so they could talk. "I love you, too," said Rebecca. Finally, just before the final hour on Sunday, it was Father's Day. Now I could go to sleep.

I had gotten a call from our older daughter, Sarah, earlier in the day. She had called me from the emergency room at Children's Hospital. She was working on Sunday, too, as a first-year resident pediatrician at Children's Hospital in Oakland. She had sent me a Father's Day card a few days earlier, telling me she was glad to have me as her No. 1 fan.

I must have done something right as a father, I thought, that both of my girls were calling me from work. Sunday is supposed to be a day of rest, but that's never been so in our house. I worked on weekends most of my life because there were always sports events to cover on Saturday and Sunday. Kathie always seems to be working.

Both of my girls were putting in long days. They usually do. That's the nature of the business they are both in. Rebecca is a manager of a newly opened restaurant in suburban Columbus, Ohio. It is called California Pizza Kitchen Restaurant and it's located in the Easton Shopping Center near her home. She is one of three managers who report to a general manager. California Pizza Kitchen is coming east. It's a trendy restaurant that features gourmet pizza and fancy sandwiches and salads. Women especially love it and the outlets are usually located in resort communities and upscale shopping centers.

Rebecca had her choice of where to train and she chose West Palm Beach, Florida. I have two smart daughters. Kathie and I had a chance to visit Rebecca in South Florida a month ago, toward the end of her 11-week training period. They had put her up in a two-bedroom apartment in a beautiful complex, provided her with airplane tickets to get there and back, including a trip home midway through her training period, along with a rental car. It's no wonder she wanted to stay there.

She celebrated her 24th birthday there on May 7, just a few days before our visit. Her sister, Dr. Sarah O'Brien-Zirwas, is 27. Sarah has been married to Dr. Matthew Zirwas for over two years now. He is a first-year resident in medicine at UPMC in Oakland. They're living in a townhouse in Oakmont.

My father, Dan O'Brien, died a year after Kathie and I were married 34 years ago. I thought about him on Sunday. I visited my mother, Mary O'Brien, now 94, on Father's Day. We sat out by the gazebo and the gardens at Asbury Heights, an assisted-care living facility in Mt. Lebanon.

"Your father had his good ways and his bad ways," she said, "but he was always good with you kids."

My mother has her good days and her bad days, and this, fortunately, was a good day. We could talk. I had a good day playing basketball that morning, as I had the previous morning. It doesn't take much to make a good day for me. My wife visited her mother and dad, who are both being challenged by health issues. She had to help her dad unwrap his Father's Day present.

He was grateful and he smiled. Kathie told him he was a good dad. That's all any man who marries and has children should need to hear: that he's a good husband, that he's a good father. That's real success. It took a while before that was finally reaffirmed for me on Sunday, but it was worth the wait.

Harvey Churchman and sister Kathie with their parents Barb and Clell during visit to Raleigh, North Carolina.

A priceless photo provides
a smile in difficult time

July 19, 2001

A third cousin of my wife Kathie made quite a discovery earlier this year. After his grandmother died, Jim Sproat was clearing out his grandmother's home in Bedford, Pennsylvania. He came across an old camera in a closet. In checking it closer, he realized it still had film in it.

He removed the film cartridge from the camera and had it developed at a film-processing outlet. It contained photos of my wife's family. Her father, Harvey Churchman, had taken the photos. He was quite a good photographer.

There were pictures of Kathie and her brother Harvey when she was seven and he was five. There was a photo of their mother. Barbara Churchman was kneeling in a flowerbed, working with flowers in her backyard, as she loved to do. She had a bright smile on her lovely face. She was 33 years old. That was 50 years ago.

She looked so happy. The family had just bought their first home in White Oak, just outside of McKeesport. It was a two-story white home with a two-car garage in the middle of a big yard on flat terrain. It cost $11,000. They say Barbara cried most of the first week after they moved into it, worrying about how they were going to pay for it.

All the photos were so sharp, so well defined; different from the color photos so standard today. It was like an archaeological find. There were several close-ups of my wife. Some showed her with a happy face, one with such a sad face. I saw both faces again last week.

Barbara Churchman lost her battle with cancer on Friday the 13th of July, 2001. She died at 1:30 a.m. in her bed in the nursing center at Asbury Heights in Mt. Lebanon, just four miles from our home in the South Hills.

Photo by Harvey Churchman

Kathie, her dad and I were with Barbara nearly all day on Thursday. I brought my mother, Mary O'Brien, who has been at Asbury Heights for over two years, into her room to see her. We knew Barbara didn't have long to live. She and her husband had come to Asbury Heights, an assisted care facility, at the outset of June following hospital stays in McKeesport. Harvey had broken his left arm in a fall at the doorstep of their home, and had fractured a pelvic bone two weeks later when he fell on the porch.

Kathie was caring for them, visiting them every night when she came home from work, looking after cancer patients and their families as a social worker at Allegheny General Hospital. "It's different when you're the daughter," Kathie said of her role.

She was doing their laundry and ironing their clothes each night. Then, three weeks ago, she fell playing tennis and broke her right arm. And she is right-handed, of course. We wondered what else could go wrong. It didn't take long to learn the answer to that question.

That black-and-white photo of Kathie's mother in her flower garden prompted many comments among the family and friends who came to pay their last respects to Barbara Churchman. It was one of about 40 photos on display.

There were photos of her as a teenager growing up in Duquesne. I had gone through scrapbooks at the Churchman home during the funeral and found newspaper clippings with stories about President Franklin Delano Roosevelt in the early 1940s. There were stories about World War II, with Germany and Japan. There was a whole section of a *Pittsburgh Sun-Telegraph*, priced at 3 cents, about the D-Day Invasion in 1944. There were clippings from *The Pittsburgh Press*, where I worked at three different periods in my life. Barbara and some of her girl friends from Duquesne appeared in a front-page picture about their participation in Croatian Day at Kennywood Park.

The family was living in Kennywood when my wife was born in 1943. That photo also reminded me that Kathie and I had our wedding reception in 1967 at the Croatian Club in Duquesne. More good memories. I remembered that Barbara Churchman wore a light blue suit with matching pillbox hat that wedding day, the kind Jackie Kennedy made popular at the time.

We would be celebrating Barbara's birthday (August 17) and my birthday (August 20) and our 34th wedding anniversary (August 12) next month. Barbara always made a big fuss to properly celebrate such occasions.

The casket was closed at Barbara's request, so the photos were even more important. Over 300 people came to the Jennifer S. Jordan Funeral Home, just across Lincoln Way in White Oak from Barbara's church, Sampson's Mills Presbyterian Church, and just three blocks from that white house where the Churchmans had lived for 50 years. She and Harvey were married for 60 years.

She had so many close friends, so many admirers. One identified them as "the Depression kids." They had values and virtues that are rare today, a wonderful work ethic, a solidarity and strength to be envied. Barbara's parents, Marko and Agata Stepetic, were born in Croatia. Agata is the Croatian version of Agatha. Barbara's dad died when she was an infant, her mother when she was in grade school. She was raised by stepparents whom she dearly loved. But it was difficult for a young child to make the adjustments. So family was always foremost in Barbara's mind.

She made sure her children, Kathie and Harvey, did the right things and went to college. She was a wonderful grandmother to our kids, Sarah and Rebecca, and to Harvey's kids, Jason and Emily.

There were a lot of photos and memories and warm stories shared in the funeral home and the Churchman home. They prompted smile and cheers. She was a good wife, a good mother and that rare good mother-in-law. We'll miss her dearly. It's good that we have the photos, the ones on display and the ones in our minds. Photos and memories, Joyce Carol Oates has written, that's what families are all about.

Bad news doesn't invade
Mom's world anymore

October 11, 2001

A new season of TV shows is upon us, and it includes "America's Response," or the Attack on Afghanistan. The television is usually turned on when I visit my mother at Asbury Heights, an assisted-care residence in Mt. Lebanon, just four miles from our home in neighboring Upper St. Clair, and about the same distance from The Point in downtown Pittsburgh.

My mother doesn't really watch it or listen to it. It's like background music. Late at night, her radio is usually turned on to a classical station with soothing music, the kind that makes it easier to get to sleep.

My mother sleeps too much these days. The images of the World Trade Center, the Pentagon and the farm field in Shanksville, near Somerset, were flashing on the TV screen during one evening visit, and I asked my mother what was going on. "Not much," she responded.

It was a dark, deeply troubling time in America. We were under attack by terrorists. In my mother's mind it was "not much." I thought there must be some comfort in that, not knowing what was transpiring.

This past Sunday the U.S. launched an aerial attack on Afghanistan and, once again, my mother had no clue as to what was going on.

She had no awareness of evil forces like Bin Laden or The Taliban. She did not know that Barry Bonds of the San Francisco Giants, the former star of the Pittsburgh Pirates, had hit a record-breaking 73 home runs or that the Pirates had lost 100 games in their first season at PNC Park.

She had always been a big sports fan, but she didn't know that the Steelers had beaten the Cincinnati Bengals in the first regular season game at Heinz Field, and that these rivals were now both 2-2 in the AFC Central standings. She didn't know Penn State was 0-4, that Pitt and Notre Dame were both 1-3, that West Virginia was 2-3, and that it had been a bad weekend for area college football fans. But I didn't envy her.

She knew my name and that usually signals a good day. Some days she doesn't know my name. "Is it Johnny?" she asked me one day a week ago. "How about if I just call you My Boy?" I could see this coming, so I shouldn't be surprised. She has a Teflon memory anymore. Nothing sticks. She still has a good appetite and doesn't miss many meals. But she has no idea what she's eating. She can't tell you a minute afterward what she had for lunch or dinner.

She smiles when she sees me. She likes to hold my hand or grasp my arm. She always tells me how good I look, and nobody else does that, which is why mothers are so special. "You're as cute as Christmas," she said one recent night.

My mother will turn 95 this Christmas Eve and I am confident she will make it. Though I don't know if that's good or not. I don't want to see her get sick or worse than she is now. Friends ask me, "How's your mother doing?" I don't know how to answer them anymore. I borrow a line she likes to use. "She's hanging in there," I say.

My mother-in-law died at age 83 in mid-July. My mother's kid sister died shortly before that, and my mother had no awareness of either event. I thought that was sad, but I saw no sense in trying to tell her. My mother forgets that my father-in-law is two doors down the hall at Asbury Heights. He is 85 and, like my mother, likes his new home. He has good days and bad days. My wife and I visit five or six days a week. It's demanding.

My mother calls out my name at night in the dark of her room, the nurses and attendants tell me. I heard her doing that one night last week when Kathie and I were coming down the hall. My mother had no idea I was there. It was disturbing. When I entered her room, she smiled and told me how glad she was to see me. She yawned as we were talking, and she placed her hand over her mouth to cover up. She might be losing her mind, I thought, but she hasn't lost her good manners. She thanks everyone for everything they do for her. That is why they love her at Asbury Heights. I'm lucky there are so many good people looking after her. I can't be there all the time.

Ghosts of Christmas past
can be found everywhere

A so-called Sister of Charity cautioned my mother during my eighth and final year at St. Stephen's Catholic Grade School in Hazelwood. "Your son," said Sister Mary Leo, "is going to end up in Sing Sing someday!"

Sister Mary Leo must have been upset with me. After all, Sing Sing was a famous prison facility in upstate New York.

When I was to graduate from the University of Pittsburgh, my mother sent Sister Mary Leo an invitation to the ceremonies. "See," my mother wrote on the card, "he didn't end up in Sing Sing after all."

This all came to mind last Friday night when I found myself in jail in downtown Pittsburgh. Sister Mary Leo must have had a smug look on her pale face somewhere above.

Then again, when I went to jail for the first time in my life I found myself in the distinguished company of Mayor Tom Murphy, State Attorney General Mike Fisher and Judge Ralph Cappy, to name a few VIPs. My mother always said you are judged by the company you keep.

They were among the hundreds present for a Christmas party hosted by Jack Mascaro, the president of Mascaro Construction on the North Side.

These are high times for Mascaro. His company is not only refurbishing the jail, but it is building the new football stadium and practice facilities for the Steelers and Pitt Panthers. Fisher and Mascaro were classmates at St. Bernard's Grade School and South Catholic High School in Mt. Lebanon. Now they live in Upper St. Clair.

213

Renowned architect Frank Lloyd Wright, while visiting Pittsburgh long ago, once said the jail was the only building in the city worth preserving. It has been converted into court rooms and judges' chambers and support offices. It's a real beauty. "This is a great save," said Judge Cappy, a former classmate of mine at Pitt.

"We're all so lucky," declared an exuberant Mascaro. "We're here with family and friends and we have so much to celebrate."

Some of the cells from the old jail have been preserved as a mini-museum, and that offered a contrasting mood, bleak images of the history of the jail. My wife Kathie and I walked through the cell area and into the cells. They are so small and so stark. There are well-stained cots and toilet facilities and angry graffiti to be found there. I felt the presence of past inhabitants of those cells. The ghosts of former inmates are still there.

"This was not a nice place," Mascaro said.

Mayor Murphy was looking forward to the next day when the Steelers would be playing their final game at Three Rivers Stadium in his neighborhood. It would be a bittersweet experience for all. I revisited Mayor Murphy in a box at Three Rivers Stadium and he was one of those who were caught up in the emotional finale. The Steelers ripped the Redskins, 24-3, and they brought out the best of the Steelers from the past, parading Hall of Famers across the field and the jumbo screen. And they had fireworks. Parades and fireworks have always been sure-fire hits in Pittsburgh.

It was an exhilarating experience for all, including those who watched on TV. I went to one of the best Christmas parties in the Pittsburgh area late that same night. Armand Dellovade, the Canonsburg industrialist, had his annual fete at his palatial home in Lawrence, and there were judges and jocks filling every room. Everybody was still buzzing about the last game at Three Rivers.

The announced comeback attempt by another Hall of Famer, Mario Lemieux of the Penguins, the final game at Three Rivers and Pitt going to a bowl game have created a buzz in the 'Burgh we haven't enjoyed in many holiday seasons. I hear talk about it in every shopping mall I visit in the tri-state area during my annual book-signing tour. There's a great spirit in the air this holiday season. There's an upbeat mood among the shoppers at the area malls I haven't felt in years.

It's a shame Steelers' founder Art Rooney wasn't there. He always enjoyed a good wake.

While driving through Homestead on my way to Waldenbooks at Century III Mall in West Mifflin last week, I went by the site of the old Mesta Machine Company. That's where my father and brother, and two of my uncles, Rich and Robbie, worked once upon a time. They are all gone now. I could see them clearly as I drove by their old workplace. It was a sad moment. I think all of us think about departed loved ones during the Christmas season. It's as much a part of the season as all the decorations, gifts and Santa Claus and images of the birth of Jesus Christ.

This past Tuesday, as is my custom, I made my annual trip to Indiana, Pa., the Christmas Tree Capital of the World. That's the hometown of Jimmy Stewart. His 1946 movie, *It's A Wonderful Life,* came to mind. It's a Christmas classic. One can still see Stewart racing down the streets of his hometown. *The Christmas Carol* isn't the only show in town with ghosts of Christmas past.

This year should be a happier year for our family

January 2, 2002

I took my daughter Rebecca's dog Bailey for a long walk on Christmas Day. It was brisk, but Bailey loves the weather that way and it seemed to sharpen my senses.

I had much to think about. It had been a difficult holiday season and it wasn't over yet. This was a test for everyone in our family.

So much had happened in a short period. It was too much to absorb in one month. There were extreme highs and lows. It was as numbing as the cold wind that blew into my face when Bailey and I returned home.

My wife's father had died three days earlier, at daybreak on Saturday. A friend and colleague from my days in New York, author and TV sports personality Dick Schaap had died from an infection during hip replacement surgery.

My father-in-law, Harvey M. Churchman Jr., was 85. He had been ill all year and had suffered a major stroke the week before. His death wasn't as shocking to me as Dick Schaap's. Schaap was 67 and looked terrific when I last saw him at the Super Bowl in Tampa.

Schaap had provided the postscript for my latest book, *The Chief — Art Rooney and his Pittsburgh Steelers*. I was pictured on the last page of the book beside Schaap. We both looked terrific.

My book had been the most successful during the holiday season of any of the 13 books I have written about Pittsburgh sports subjects. It was the No. 1 selling "regional" book in the entire Eastern region in the Waldenbooks chain. It was No. 3 overall in this area, right behind John Grisham's *Skipping Christmas* and James Patterson's *Violets Are Blue*.

216

I drew little joy from that achievement. I was torn emotionally. My wife, Kathie, was hurting. Her mother, Barbara Churchman, had died in mid-July at age 84. In a space of six months, Kathie had lost her mother and her father. They were so dedicated to her and her younger brother, Harvey. In turn, they were dedicated to their parents. My daughters, Sarah and Rebecca, had lost their grandma and grandpap in one swoop in 2001.

My mother, Mary O'Brien, turned 95 on Christmas Eve. After my walk on Christmas Day, Kathie and I went over to Asbury Heights, the assisted-care facility in Mt. Lebanon, to bring Christmas presents to my mother. Her room was on the same floor as where Kathie's parents had resided during the year. Barbara was there only a month, but Harvey had settled in, made good friends and was a favorite among the staff. He was a gentle man, soft-spoken, reserved and easygoing. People liked him.

So there were ghosts on that floor for Kathie, but she went with me, even though she knew it would be a challenge. My mother's mind is muddled these days. She knows Kathie and me and, for some reason, Bailey. But she gets my girls mixed up. I told her, for the second time in as many days, that Kathie's father had died. Still, it was a surprise to her.

Kathie had to go to her dad's former room to pick up something. As she returned, I told my mother to say something to her about her dad dying. As Kathie approached, my mother looked up at her and smiled. "Happy Birthday, Kathie," my mother said.

Kathie couldn't help but smiling. "It's your birthday, Mom," she said. "Not mine."

It was good to see her smile. The funeral service for her father was the day after Christmas. Kathie kept smiling when she saw her aunts and cousins and the many friends of her parents. The funeral home and the setting were so familiar. It seemed like only the week before that we were there for her mother. They had so many friends who spoke well of them.

That was comforting. But Kathie and our family always knew that her parents were special, that we were so lucky to have them. It snowed and there was snow on the ground for the first time all year the day we buried Harvey Churchman. I wondered why that happened. What did God have in mind? Hopefully, there will be sunnier days in 2003.

Kathie and her dad help her mom celebrate birthday.

> *"Life is either a daring adventure or nothing."*
> **— Helen Keller**

You're never alone when you are grieving over a loss

January 10, 2002

I am grateful for the folks in our neighborhood who have kept their Christmas lights and decorations on display past the traditional holiday season.

I was walking my daughter Rebecca's dog Bailey in our neighborhood on Sunday night, around 10 o'clock, after the big snowfall. It was the best the neighborhood had looked all during the holiday season. If you didn't have to drive anywhere, it was a great scene.

The snow reflected the lights as well as a big moon and no matter which way you looked there was a great scene that could be a Christmas card.

I had missed much of the holiday scene because I was part of it, signing books every day for a month at area shopping malls, and because of the illness and death of my father-in-law, Harvey M. Churchman Jr. He died, as you may have read here, the Saturday morning before Christmas at Asbury Heights in Mt. Lebanon.

He was born in Homestead 85 years ago and lived most of his life in McKeesport and White Oak. He had worked as an electrical tester at Westinghouse Electric Corp. in East Pittsburgh for over 35 years before retiring 20 years ago. He was a good man and we missed him dearly the past few weeks.

We were not alone. Our next-door neighbor on one side of our home, Claudia Franyutti, and her family rushed to Oklahoma on Christmas Day where her kid sister, age 53, died the same day. She had never recovered from a devastating auto accident two years earlier.

Our neighbor on the other side, Nancy Moore, lost her father, at age 73, to a bout with cancer a few days before my Kathie's dad died. The Moores were in the process of moving to a new home nearby during Christmas Week.

We learned via e-mail from Helen and Dan Caldwell, who had lived in that same home before the Moores did, that their long-time neighbor Carl Saalbach had died on Dec. 27 at Friendship Village where he had moved earlier in the year. So there were deaths during the holidays involving people in four homes in one patch of ground in our neighborhood.

"My own mother passed away on Christmas Eve in 1981," wrote Helen Caldwell from her home near Cary, North Carolina, "and every Christmas Eve since among the joys of family, friends, wrappings and gifts that sad loss is deeply felt even more."

At church earlier that Sunday, we learned that a couple we know had suffered the loss of a 2½-year-old granddaughter on Christmas Day. The little girl, who was born with a defective heart, had to be rushed from their home to Canonsburg Hospital where she died.

As difficult as our loss had been, coming on the heels of the death of Kathie's mother six months earlier, we knew that we could bear our setback easier than one like that.

I am always amazed at the personal stuff people share with me at booksignings during the holidays. A woman at South Hills Village told me she had just completed a round of chemotherapy treatments for breast cancer, but was hopeful her health would improve this year.

A woman at Ross Park Mall told me she was working for United Way in Butler, which helped her get over a difficult year. I told her that our family had also had a difficult year. Then she disclosed that her four-year-old son had drowned during the summer. I didn't know what to say.

"I have no idea of how you must feel," I said.

So many people experience great losses and setbacks, and they are only more poignant and more deeply felt during the holidays, which are supposed to be a time of tidings and joy. Everyone in this country, perhaps the world, was more fragile after the tragic events of September 11. That's why we need to listen when people tell us their problems. Sometimes they just need to talk to somebody.

"It's faith, and the comfort offered by family and friends," said the grandfather of that little girl who died on Christmas Day, "that enables us to get through these losses."

Sarah, Matt and Rebecca join Jim, Kathie and Bailey for Christmas celebration.

Every visit to Mom now is on Valentine's Day

February 21, 2002

I can't have a real conversation with my mother anymore. She can't find the answers to my questions. "I don't know," she says. "I don't remember."

She smiles when she sees me and there's a glint in her soft blue moist eyes. She smiles a lot. I have learned to be content with that, and whatever else she has to offer. Usually, she resorts to saying the same things, repeatedly. They are compliments, so I suppose I am lucky.

She says the kinds of things one expects to find in a Hallmark greeting card. It's like getting a belated Valentine's Day card.

"It's always a pleasure to see you," she begins. They come about every five minutes during an hour-long visit.

"You're so good looking."

"You're looking better than ever."

"I could look at you all day."

"I love you more than words can say."

"I love you, I love you, I love you," she says, almost in a song.

She is sitting in her wheel chair in the middle of Main Street, a sun-splashed oasis in the center of the campus complex that is Asbury Heights, an assisted-care facility in Mt. Lebanon. There's an ice cream and sandwich shop, a confectionery store, hair-styling salons and a post office and chapel on Main Street. It's almost a stage setting from a movie.

Other residents and employees pass by and say hello, and pat my mother on the back, hold her hand — they often express their surprise at her firm handshake — and offer kind words. She always says, "Thank you" and smiles, and asks if they've met her son.

"I'm so proud of you," she frequently says.

When I told her I was going to be 60 this summer, she said, "You don't look it."

It's one compliment after another. Trust me, I don't believe what she's saying, but it's nice to hear it anyway. No one but your mother will say those sorts of things. I will miss those words someday.

Then she added, "I think I'm having a birthday today."

When I asked her how old she was, she said, "I guess I'm close to 65. I'm not as old as I am, though."

"If you're 65," I said, "you can retire."

"No, I can't retire," she said. "I gotta live."

She lives in the nursing center at Asbury Heights. I haven't been able to call her on the telephone for about two years now because she can't use a telephone anymore. She is hard of hearing. The hearing aids help on some days, not always.

She looks fine, she feels fine, nothing bothers her. She turned 95 on Christmas Eve. She has been diagnosed with dementia, which isn't as bad as Alzheimer's Disease. She retains little information. When I reminded her that my Kathie's parents had both died this past year, it was news to her all over again. "That's too bad," she said.

"How's your family doing?" she asked me at one point.

When I told her, she followed with another question, "And how's your mother?"

Celebrating Mother's Day
in a very special way

May 15, 2002

It was more than just a walk in the park. It was an educational field trip. This was the 10th annual Susan G. Komen Breast Cancer Foundation Race For The Cure at Schenley Park this past Sunday, which was fittingly Mother's Day as well. The Pittsburgh event has raised over $6 million to help women with breast cancer awareness, education and early detection.

My wife, Kathie, asked me to accompany her this year, her fifth time around the block and back. This event has always been meaningful to her because she has worked with cancer patients and their families during that same ten-year time span as a social worker in the oncology unit at Allegheny General Hospital.

This time it was particularly poignant and heartfelt because her mother, Barbara Churchman, had died from breast cancer in mid-July, a month short of her 84th birthday.

As soon as we arrived at the assembly area on Flagstaff Hill I felt a rush of sadness come over me. We picked up pink sheets to sign and wear on our backs. Kathie chose the right sheet to fill out, the one that read "In Memory Of..." In my haste, I picked up the wrong sheet. It said "In Celebration Of..." Mine was for those who are living the good fight against cancer.

I kept mine. It's important to celebrate the lives of those we've lost, rather than mourn them. And who wants to admit they've made a mistake? Tears filled my eyes as I filled out the form. Thinking about my mother-in-law and about how much Kathie missed her, and how Mother's Day made that absence even more painful. Tears were coming down Kathie's cheeks as well.

Over 38,000 showed up to demonstrate their support for this program aimed at raising funds to defeat what one speaker referred to as "that awful disease."

Most of them had written in the names of mothers, sisters, aunts, friends and loved ones that had succumbed to cancer or were dealing with the challenges of cancer treatment and care. Seeing all those names on Mother's Day had a real impact. It made a more dramatic statement about how many people in Pittsburgh and its surrounding environs have been impacted by cancer.

I had gone to Flagstaff Hill as a high school student with my biology class for a field trip in its woods, and I had gone there to set up the starting and finishing line for cross-country meets. The latter came to mind when the women in pink outfits lined up for the Survivors Parade in a roped-off path.

There were over 2,200 "survivors" who had registered for the 5K, or 3.5 mile walk. There was also a 5K race earlier in the morning. Over 300 of these women participated in a parade across Flagstaff Hill, walking past people who applauded them as they went. It was the most dramatic aspect of the day.

They wore pink ballcaps, pink T-shirts and pink gloves. Most of them wore happy faces as well. I didn't want them to see me with tears in my eyes because they don't want you to feel sorry for them. The woman standing in front of me had tears in her eyes, too. Lots of people did.

A woman broke ranks in the parade and came over to the woman in front of me. "We're OK," she said to comfort her. "It's OK."

Children's Hospital was visible in the distance. Our older daughter, Sarah, couldn't accompany her mother this year because she was working the overnight shift at Children's. Sarah has told us she wants to pursue a career in pediatric oncology. As a father, you want to advise her to take up something that might be a little more fun. She has a chance to be a doctor who can make a difference, however, and that would be so satisfying and rewarding. It would also be challenging and heart-breaking at times.

She and her sister Rebecca miss their grandmother very much. Barbara Churchman was with us as we walked through Schenley Park. In a different way, we were with her on Mother's Day.

Kathie is flanked by her parents, Clell and Barbara Churchman.

A memorable interview
with Ted Williams

July 10, 2002

A lot of people regarded Ted Williams as one of America's greatest sports heroes. Others, mindful of his five years of military service as a Marine Corps pilot in World War II and Korea, considered him one of our greatest heroes.

Others thought he was a pain in the butt. He was a headstrong, often difficult individual and he had a long-standing feud with some of the fans at Fenway Park in Boston and with the media.

For me, Williams was both. He was the last major leaguer to have a .400 batting average — hitting .406 in 1941 — and his lifetime batting average was .344. That was in 19 seasons with the Red Sox. He missed five seasons, three of them at the peak of his playing career, when he was called up for military service. He died last Friday at age 83 in Florida.

I had a one-on-one interview with Williams in March of 1969 and I've never forgotten it. I was 27 and in my first week as a sportswriter with *The Miami News*. Williams was 51 and in his first spring training camp as manager of the Washington Senators.

My wife Kathie and I were midway through our second year of marriage when we moved from Pittsburgh to Miami. We were staying in a motel that first week, waiting for an apartment to be readied for us. I was assigned to go to Pompano Beach to interview Williams, perhaps the greatest hitter in the history of baseball.

I was eager and nervous about the prospect of talking to one of the legendary figures in sports history.

He was known to be a difficult interview at times and didn't suffer sportswriters too well. On the eve of the interview, I was having a difficult time breathing as I tried to sleep in our motel room. It got so bad that Kathie decided to take me to a nearby hospital.

I had grown up in the Glenwood-Hazelwood section in the heart of the Smoky City, downwind from a slaughter house across the Monongahela River in Hays and I was having a hard time breathing in Miami. The salt air from the ocean is intoxicating for most, but I couldn't breathe. I wasn't used to clean air.

At the hospital, a nurse gave me a shot in the butt that hurt so badly it brought tears to my eyes. It felt like she had tossed a spear in my backside. It still hurt the next day. When I think about it I swear it still hurts today. It felt like an alligator had gotten a grip on my behind and wouldn't let go.

Kathie wanted to help me so she drove me to Pompano Beach that day. I couldn't sit up straight to drive myself. I was in the passenger seat, tilted somewhat. I was sitting on one cheek with a pillow propped under the other cheek. I had tears on my other cheeks.

When we got to Pompano Beach, I was still hurting. I wanted to beg off. "We came all this way," Kathie scolded. "You get out and do the interview."

I dried my eyes so Williams wouldn't know I was in distress. The pain kept me occupied so I wasn't as nervous as I might have been. Williams was new to managing, but knew that he was expected to be more public-relations conscious in his new role. And he was.

He couldn't have been better. He smiled throughout the interview, and was generous with his time and thoughts. He had always been known as one of the game's greatest analysts with a remarkable memory.

Williams mellowed in his later years and he stole the show at the All-Star Game in Boston in 1999 when he appeared in a golf cart to join the greatest players of the century who were present. He had become an ambassador for the game.

Bob Friend, one of my all-time favorite Pirates, struck out Williams with the bases loaded in the 1956 Major League All-Star Game in Washington, D.C.

Friend threw him an outside curve ball on a full count for the final out of his three-inning stint. "I remember the pitch because it was against Ted Williams in an All-Star Game," offered Friend.

He bumped into Williams 15 years later, walking through the airport with his son, Bobby Jr., in Atlanta, and introduced himself to Williams. "I don't know if you remember me or not," Friend said.

"I remember you," Williams said. "You know, I never thought you'd curve me."

Photo by Sharon Pociask

Jim and Kathie mark wedding anniversary.

Milestones are reminders
of a road well traveled

August 7, 2002

I circled two dates on my August calendar. Kathie and I will celebrate our 35th wedding anniversary on August 12. I will be marking my 60th birthday on August 20. I'm prouder of the first; it's an achievement. The second just happened, and I have a hard time believing it to be so.

I was a lucky young man the day I discovered Kathie. It was at a party in Oakland when we were both in graduate school at the University of Pittsburgh. Kathie was completing her studies for a master's degree in social work, and I was taking some post-graduate Literature classes after coming out of a two-year commitment in the U.S. Army.

Kathie has kept me on my toes, and sometimes my heels, ever since. She has had the greatest impact on my life of anyone I have known.

Kathie is demanding and often difficult to please. She set the highest standards for our daughters, Sarah and Rebecca, and for me, and we have all benefited from that. She keeps the three of us humble.

I came back a week ago from speaking at the grand opening of a new library in Plum Borough and told Kathie that a woman told me she could listen to me all night. Kathie came back, "I do, and it's no great shakes."

Our house has been in an upheaval in recent weeks as we had some painting and wallpapering done in rooms upstairs. I couldn't find my wedding ring for two days and I got anxious about its absence. I didn't tell Kathie because I didn't want her giving me any flak. This is my third wedding ring. Kathie keeps track of stuff like that. When I finally relented and told her, she told me that she had put it away in my dresser. When I saw the ring it was like finding the ring of power in *The Lord of the Rings*. I was out de-thatching our front yard — raking the dead stuff out of the grass — when Kathie came upon me, probably to inspect my work. It was a task she had been after me to do the last three years.

I told her I had a story to tell her. A fellow from Brookline named Barry Gordon, who was retired from being the head groundskeeper at Three Rivers Stadium, had died the day before. One of his sons told me they put a copy of my book on Art Rooney, *The Chief*, in their dad's coffin because he was so proud of the chapter I had written about him in the book.

I told Kathie that was the fourth casket I knew of that one of my books had been placed in for the funeral service. Kathie came back, "I'll tell you another casket your book is going to be in...your casket! When you go, all your stuff in the garage is going with you. There will be a few boxes of books in your casket."

See what I mean. Kathie keeps me humble, and on the straight and narrow. Sometimes I wish she'd let me up for air. Sometimes I feel like I'm walking through a minefield, afraid of a misstep.

The saving grace is I realize that her discipline has been good for me. It has kept me out of trouble for the most part.

Our daughter Sarah sent me an e-mail last week in which she said she was surprised that I referred to us as "seniors" in my last column. I told Sarah that, like it or not, we are, indeed, seniors. We have had our AARP cards for a couple of years, we get senior discounts at stores, hotels and movie theaters. I've got a 95-year-old mother, and that's a reminder that I'm not a kid anymore. More people call me "Mr. O'Brien" these days.

Kathie keeps our home and me clean and looking our best at all times. She even irons my T-shirts and undershorts.

That puts her in my Hall of Fame right there. I went to the Pro Football Hall of Fame last Saturday to see John Stallworth of the Steelers and Jim Kelly of East Brady and the Buffalo Bills get inducted.

Everyone spoke about the important role their families had played in their success. The inductees were all grateful for the support they had received through the years. It reminds me of how lucky I have been.

Stallworth and the Steelers of the '70s always speak about having those four Super Bowl rings, and how that is a testament to their success. If I hadn't found that wedding ring last month I might have had my fourth wedding ring by now.

Stallworth is still married to Flo, and they are one of the few couples from those Steelers of the '70s who remain married. Kathie has a locket from the Steelers' fourth Super Bowl triumph, back when I was covering the club for *The Pittsburgh Press*, and she still has her first wedding ring. I'm glad it's the one I gave her. To me, my wedding ring is better than any Super Bowl ring.

Jim and Kathie show off rings on wedding day, August 12, 1967.

Cousins come together for reunion on an idyllic farm

August 21, 2002

A picture is supposed to be worth a thousand words. It was, indeed, when my wife's cousins held a reunion last Saturday. Everyone brought family photographs, but one in particular sparked the most conversation. It was one of Kathie and five of her cousins sitting alongside each other on a low wall. Most of them were two years old at the time, one about four, the other five. They looked like Spanky McFarland and Alfalfa and "Our Gang."

Most of them had not seen each other since a funeral, and some had not seen each other in as many as 15 or 20 years. Many are in their late 50s or early 60s now, but for one day they were all kids again.

Once upon a time, they would see each other every weekend, after church, and during holidays, especially Christmas, and at family picnics. They were so close when they were growing up in places like Kennywood, West Mifflin, Munhall, Duquesne, McKeesport and North Versailles.

Now they came from as far away as New Mexico and North Carolina, Virginia and Maryland, and some from White Oak, Upper St. Clair and Robinson Township. They gathered on a mostly sunny day on an idyllic 50-acre farm in West Sunbury, just above Butler. Joanne and Ken Matthews own the farm. She was Joanne Carr when she grew up in Duquesne. Her dad, Sam Carr, was well known in the community. He looked after all the ball fields. Now she and her husband and their kids looked after farm fields. Their farm is better maintained than most backyard gardens.

It took an hour and a half to drive there. It was a trip back in time, to the '50s and '60s, and no one showed their AARP membership cards when they opened their wallets to show more family photos. The corn and tomatoes and peppers and herbs came fresh from their fields and the food was terrific. So was the IC Light and Rolling Rock so everybody would remember their roots. Before I left home, I pumped up a pro-model football and grabbed a baseball and some gloves. I thought we could at least pass the football around, or play pitch-and-catch with the baseball. But no one touched them.

I was three days away from my 60th birthday and trying to fend off getting old by playing ball. Everyone, however, was content to sit around and pass around pictures and stories, identifying whoever wasn't familiar to some one.

For the spouses, it was a chance to learn more about the family they had joined. Kathie's mother, Barbara Churchman, kept in close touch with all her nieces and nephews through the years. She was good about that. She would have celebrated her 85th birthday last Sunday. She would have been proud to know that Kathie had been the catalyst for this reunion, and that her son, Harvey Churchman Jr., was there, too. Joanne Matthews and Betty Jane Peckman joined Kathie in putting this gathering together.

Kathie lost her mother last July and her father in December. It was the most difficult year in Kathie's life. Her parents both died at Asbury Heights, an assisted-care residence in Mt. Lebanon. These were all cousins on her mother's side of the family.

Everybody at the reunion remembered their own parents; most of them have died as well. And they remembered favorite aunts and uncles. They remembered Christmases past, and family folklore. They caught their cousins up to date with what their families were doing.

I have always enjoyed my wife's family reunions more than some members of their family. I envied them their closeness. I see my cousins when I am doing book-signings at South Hills Village and Century III Mall. When I was a kid, I don't remember ever visiting anyone that was not a relative. But we haven't had a reunion in over 30 years.

It seemed like a lifetime, to this impatient photographer anyhow, as we tried to duplicate that photo of the six cousins on the wall at this farm near Butler. Everybody sat in the same position, from left to right, and took their cues from the childhood photo to pose in a certain way, and the cameras kept clicking.

If there's anything we all ought to have learned at this gathering it should be the importance of family pictures. Most of our memories are not of actual events, but more so of the photos that preserve those events. This was a good idea. Having a family reunion like this is well worth the effort.

Cousins get together in summer of 2002: Tim Stepetic, Joanne Matthews, Bobbie Carr, Kathie O'Brien, Lou Goldman and Betty Jane Peckman at Matthews' farm in West Sunbury, ten miles north of Butler. Bottom shot shows them a few years earlier in identical lineup.

Christmas season was always busy with my mother

December 19, 2002

I can't believe my mother will be 96 this Christmas Eve. But she was born on Dec. 24, 1906, so it must be true. I am still interviewing her all the time, trying to find out information about family and friends, but her mind is quite selective in what it is willing to release. My dad drank too much and smoked too much, and that contributed to his death at age 63. Mom remembers that, but all she'll say now is, "I always loved him. He always loved you kids. He never left us."

Some years back, I wasn't impressed with that appraisal. But the more mothers I meet at book-signings whose husbands no longer are a part of the family I realize that my Dad not leaving us was a plus in my life. I knew that my mother and my father loved me. They had their moles, but they never thought I had any.

"He didn't drive, but he took you kids to a lot of places," she'd say.

"He always went to work," she'd continue. "During the Depression, he didn't have a job for about six or seven years. But he went out every day and knocked on doors, and asked for work. He'd do whatever he could do to make some money. He always brought home some money."

That story has become my personal mantra. I've never been afraid to knock on doors, and ask for work. And I still smile, and think of Mom's story, when I come home with some money. It's become something of a game, and I have an inner smile and good thoughts about my mom and dad when I do it.

This was always a busy time of the year for both of my parents. My dad went to a lot of parties at this time of year. Most of those parties were held in neighborhood bars and speakeasies. There were 36 bars in a mile-long stretch between Hazelwood Avenue and the Glenwood Bridge in my hometown. My Dad was familiar with most of them, and ran a tab in a half dozen of them. I delivered newspapers to most of them, from the time I was ten to the time I was 13, so the bar owners knew me, too. I was Dan's son. They treated me well. Someone always bought me an orange soda or root beer, with some potato chips or popcorn.

When my dad cashed his paycheck from Mesta Machine Company in West Homestead at the Hazelwood Bank at one end of town, he walked, not always steadily, a veritable minefield on his way home. He had to leave a lot of that money at many of those bars to clear his account. My mother never knew how much he'd be turning over to her by the time he reached our door. Sometimes, she acted as if she'd hit the numbers; sometimes she was saddened by the shortfall.

This was a busy time of year for my mother as well. She worked as a sales clerk at the State Store on Second Avenue. My dad and mother were both good workers. This was the busiest time at the State Store. Everybody was buying liquor and wine to celebrate the season.

I met many interesting characters whenever I'd go to the State Store to see my mother. She worked a swing shift, and I'd join her for lunch on the days she worked the early shift. Sometimes I'd have to wait in the back, between the tall rows of whiskey and wine, and I'd read the labels. Many were quite attractive.

Some customers came regularly and were well known. There was "Duffy the Drunk" and "Duffy the Boxer," and a woman with scraggly dishwater gray hair known as "Swing and Sway" for her walking motion. The unkind critics would say she was staggering. The winos would bum money outside the State Store till they had enough money to buy some Tiger Rose. Mom and I went to lunch in local restaurants. To me, Isaly's was The Colony or LeMont of Hazelwood. The waitresses all knew my Mom and me. It started a lifetime of my mother and I going to lunch together. "I don't think you and your mother ever see each other that you're not eating," my wife Kathie would say, sarcastically, of course.

It was at this time of year, when I was nine years old, that I asked my mother to buy me a toy printing press, an Ace model, when we were Christmas shopping at the Hazelwood Variety Store. That's how I got started in this business. My mother never turned me down. She always believed in me even when she shouldn't have. She was always my biggest fan. I miss the mother of my childhood. Her memory isn't so good anymore. She knows me, most of the time, anyhow. I'm her Jimmy, her boy. "You're looking good," she says, over and over. "You're as cute as Christmas."

Mary O'Brien does proofreading for *Pittsburgh Weekly Sports* back in 1963.

Be sure to have a good book
and a Scrabble board, too

February 20, 2003

A fellow in Connecticut wrapped his entire home in plastic sheeting last week. That was his response to the government's latest warning about possible terrorism in this country. Anyone who saw the pictures of the man's white house on TV or in the newspapers might have thought this fellow would have been better off if he had painted the place instead. Paint had chipped off the surface in large swaths.

He wasn't the only one taking drastic measures. Many responded by doing what was suggested and stored up on canned goods, plastic sheeting, duct tape, propane heaters, flashlights, battery-operated radios, batteries and bottled water.

I have made confessions here on several occasions about my misadventures as a handyman, or fixing anything around the house. No one who works in a local hardware store would recognize me. I've screwed up enough home projects to know it's better to pay someone to do it, or to call upon my nice neighbors who take pride in their handyman abilities. I'm fortunate in that respect. Ron Temple and Sergio Franyutti are in my personal Hall of Fame for favors they have rendered. My son-in-law, Dr. Matt Zirwas, often brings a tool kit when he visits our home.

Here's a tip-off on my ignorance about this stuff. Until this week, I thought it was duck tape, not duct tape. So I can thank former Governor Tom Ridge, the pride of Munhall who heads up the national security office, for making me a little smarter.

If I got anywhere near duct tape, or duck tape, I'd end up looking like a mummified King Tut or, at least, a dead duck. For me, the end of the world would be having to measure and cut plastic sheeting and somehow get it affixed to the frames around my windows.

On the other hand, I'm not a rocket scientist but it seems to me that if I ever succeeded in closing off all the open spaces around my windows and the vents in the attic, the chimney, etc., I would end up suffocating my dear wife, Kathie, and me. Don't you need some ventilation to get air necessary to breathe? (Soon after I wrote this column, I read a story about a family that suffocated in a room they had sealed off in their house.)

Jack Boyd, owner of Rogers Hardware in Castle Shannon, said he was selling ten times the usual amount of plastic sheeting, duct tape and flashlights. He said one woman told him she had also bought a lot of canned goods, especially baked beans, to store in a room in the house that had no windows. "I told her I wouldn't want to be trapped in there," said Boyd. That part I understand.

I've never had a flashlight that didn't dim about a minute after you turned it on. I haven't listened to a battery-operated radio since Bob Prince died. Most of us got a taste of what it would be like to be penned up in our homes with our loved ones this week. Kathie and I stayed in most of Sunday because of the snowstorm. There was little that interested us on TV so we spent some part of the day reading books and we played four games of Scrabble.

We haven't done that since the early days of our marriage, before we had kids. Those were the days when we stayed up late and slept in late. We played Scrabble all the time in our apartments in Pittsburgh, Miami and then New York. We kept scoring records — that's the sportswriter in me — that we have maintained till this day.

Eventually, our daughters' names appeared in those records. And my mother, Mary O'Brien, shows up now and then, in games played in all of our apartments, wherever we went. Some of her scores were recorded 30 years ago. Seeing her scores had a bittersweet effect on me. It reminded me of when her mind was still sharp.

She's 96 now and she recently had to be relocated to a different unit at Asbury Heights, the personal care complex in Mt. Lebanon where she has been living the last five years. She's in a unit with people who have dementia, and require more attention.

Neither Kathie nor I are running to the hardware store, but we are going to take a few precautions, just in case. These government warnings are unsettling, so are the troop movements, so is the news that North Korea can launch a bomb that could hit our West Coast. Our daughter Rebecca is now living in Southern California. So now I have something else to worry about, in addition to earthquakes and California kooks. "If anything happens in the way of terrorism here," says Kathie, "I want to be wherever your mother is. No matter what happens, she'll come out of it alive."

Gathering at Emerald Isle, North Carolina for Churchman family wedding in October, 2003. Jim, Kathie, Sarah, Matt, Quinn and Rebecca.

It kept you younger
to be somebody's 'good kid'

March 1, 2003

I awoke with a start around 3:30 on Saturday morning. I went downstairs to the kitchen and had a glass of orange juice. Then I wrote some notes on a pad about my mother, and went back to bed. I was startled from my sleep by a ringing at 5:30 a.m. At first, I thought it was the alarm clock. Then I recognized that it was the telephone ringing in the next room. I thought it might be our daughter Rebecca calling from California, forgetting the three-hour time difference. Then I knew better.

I knew it was somebody calling from Asbury Heights, a senior-care complex in Mt. Lebanon where my mother has been living the last four years or so. A nurse or attendant told me she was sorry to have to tell me that my mother had died about two hours earlier. She must have died when I was up at 3:30.

It hurt to hear that, but I knew it was coming and I knew it was for the best. My mother, Mary O'Brien, was in her 96th year. She got tired of struggling and died in her sleep, the way she prayed she would. She was not in pain or distress. Her heart simply wore out. She had gotten great use out of it.

She had given us plenty of signs that she was about to die, starting nearly a month earlier. She became less communicative, less cooperative. She stopped eating, a sure sign something was amiss. She stopped smiling. She stopped saying "Thank you" every time somebody did the slightest thing for her.

Those of you who have been reading this column through the years know about my mother. She was smart,

242

but she led a simple life, and kept mostly to herself and her family. She had a chameleon-like quality, being something different to each of her four children. She was the mother each of us needed.

She taught me how to spell, to watch my grammar, to be respectful of my elders, to hold the door open for the person walking behind you, to say "thank you" when somebody did something for you. Her greatest quality was she never complained. I never picked up on that quality. I was often told I looked like my mother.

I was born at 3:36 a.m. Aug. 20, 1942. "You kept me up that first night and many nights after that," she often told me. She would call me at 3:36 a.m. on my birthday through the years, just to get back at me.

I was urged to come and see her on Friday because she was fading. Whoever had dressed her the day before she died did so thoughtfully. Mom was wearing a white jersey that my wife Kathie and I had gotten her for Mother's Day a few years back. There were pretty butterflies and flowers embroidered on the front of it. A message read: "A mother is somebody you never outgrow your need for."

My sister, Mary Carole Cook of Green Tree, had been in to see her that morning. I spent two hours with my mother that afternoon. Her eyes were closed the whole time. Once in a while they would open just a little, but there was no gleam to be seen. She was breathing heavily. She didn't say a word. I just held her hand. I told her I was there, but she showed no sign of recognition.

I had learned from an earlier experience with my mother-in-law, Barbara Churchman, of what was going on. Barbara had died at Asbury Heights nearly two years earlier. The Hospice Family & Palliative Care people in Mt. Lebanon had given us books explaining the death process. It was so helpful. It helped you read the signs and understand what was going on. Her husband, Harvey Churchman, died there six months later.

The staff at Asbury showed heartfelt concern when the word got out that my mother wasn't doing well. Some visited her to say goodbye. "She was a real sweetie, we've missed her," said a woman who looked after my mother in a different wing a few years earlier. "I liked your mother a lot," said another. "She was a delight to look after."

A nurse told my wife Kathie that she had looked after her father on the night shift. "He was a special gentleman," she said. That was good for her to hear. That helped, too.

My mother didn't want any public viewing or funeral service. So this was my first e-mail funeral. I alerted family and friends out of town by e-mail that my mother died, and they expressed sympathy and condolences by return e-mail. I stayed home most of the weekend with my thoughts and memories, and watched basketball games.

When she was still talking and still smiling, I visited her one day at Asbury Heights last month. After I returned her to the circle where she sat with fellow residents, I walked down the hall to leave. I overheard a nurse or an attendant tell someone, "He's a writer." Then I heard my mother pipe up and interject, "And he's a good kid, too!"

I smiled. As long as she's alive, I thought, I'm still somebody's kid. And, in her blue eyes anyhow, a good kid at that.

Mary O'Brien stands tall on Butler Street in Lawrenceville.

Sunny Southern California is someplace special, too

May 14, 2003

A week's stay in sunny Southern California helped me better understand why Ben Howland left Pitt in favor of UCLA and why our daughter Rebecca went west as well.

My wife Kathie and I traveled to Los Angeles for an eight-day stay to be with our younger daughter Rebecca when she celebrated her 26th birthday on May 7. I read something when I was there that there is a perception in this country that a person is considered an adult when they turn 26. To us, Rebecca is a wonderful young woman, but she is still our baby.

We hadn't seen her or her dog Bailey since early February when she moved from Columbus, Ohio, to Woodland Hills, a community about an hour's drive northwest of Los Angeles. We were also eager to spend more time with her fiancée, Quinn Carlson, who grew up in nearby Bel Air and returned with ambitions to land some movie and commercial assignments. I call Quinn the "Prince of Bel Air."

We wanted to see Rebecca's garden apartment and her new restaurant in the California Pizza Kitchen chain. This one was in Tarzana, within 15 minutes of her apartment. Now we can better picture her in her new surroundings.

While there, I also wanted to retrace some locations where the Steelers spent time when they won their last Super Bowl at the outset of 1980, and where I spent time when I first visited Los Angeles in 1970 when the Knicks knocked off the Lakers to win their first NBA title.

I thought I'd check out UCLA as well. Ben Howland was away on business, so I didn't get a chance to see him. As I stood in the center of the athletic complex on the UCLA campus I could understand why he left a great job at the University of Pittsburgh to go there.

I stood near buildings named after John Wooden and Arthur Ashe, who both left their mark there, watching the passing students, and I knew that this was also someplace special. And, for Howland, it had the hometown advantage. Like Quinn Carlson, he was born and got his start here, and he wanted to come home. His parents were there, and they were getting old, and he wanted to spend more time with them while he could. The UCLA campus is beautiful.

It was actually cooler in southern California than it was in Pittsburgh during our stay, but over the course of the year you can't beat the weather there. Winters in Pittsburgh, especially this year, are hard to bear.

Sometimes we are awfully parochial in Pittsburgh, and we think it's the only place to live. We complain that our children can't get jobs and stay here. Hey, some of our children, much to our chagrin, want to live elsewhere. Our Rebecca has long spoken of her desire to live in a warmer climate, like Florida or California. She can always come home if that attraction wears off. Right now, she likes living and working in California. The problem is we can't drive there and back in the same day as we could when she was living in Columbus.

I visited Pauley Pavilion while I was at the UCLA campus. I watched some of the Bruins' basketball players working out in the dimly lit building. No, it's not as new or as nice as the Petersen Events Center. But there are 11 NCAA basketball championship banners hanging in the rafters. I could still see Kareem Abdul-Jabbar, when he was Lew Alcindor, and Bill Walton and those other wonderful Bruins playing under the watchful eye of John Wooden. I saw all the books about Wooden at the campus bookstore. He still comes to the campus on occasion. We enjoyed our visit. We took long walks with Bailey on the flattest terrain and noted the green green grass, and how clean it was in Woodland Hills. There are lined garbage cans on every corner. All the avenues seem to have six lanes and it's a fast-paced world.

The Los Angeles Times is truly one of America's great newspapers, and there were investigative stories already examining the UCLA basketball program. It will be demanding for Ben Howland and Rebecca O'Brien. It agrees with them so far, and we're wishing them both the best of luck. We hope they're happy and successful there.

We'll miss Howland because he is such a fine coach, but Pitt will survive somehow without him. We'll miss Rebecca even more. Our daughter Sarah stopped by when we returned over the weekend to bring Kathie her Mother's Day present. Kathie had to go to California to get her Mother's Day present from Rebecca. It won't be easy, but we'll survive this countrywide separation somehow.

Quinn Carlson and Rebecca O'Brien became engaged in southern California.

Yes, there's a doctor in the church

June 4, 2003

Our daughter Sarah and her husband, Dr. Matthew Zirwas, will be celebrating their fifth wedding anniversary this June 27. They are a great couple and they complement each other well. They met during orientation week at Medical School at the University of Pittsburgh nearly seven years ago and it seems like they've been a winning parlay ever since.

Sarah is finishing her three-year residency in pediatrics at Children's Hospital in Oakland this month, and in July she will begin a three-year fellowship in oncology. She will be a pediatric oncologist, doctoring children with cancer. That should be a real challenge.

Matt is finishing the third of a four-year residency in dermatology at UPMC. One of his mentors and boosters, Dr. Mark Ceraly of McMurray, believes he has an outstanding future in the field.

To fully appreciate this story, you have to understand that Matt loves to play doctor. My wife Kathie has several aunts who love to let Matt play doctor. They are quick to show him their latest moles or skin rashes. Matt smiles and checks them out. Sarah smiles and stays in the background. She saves her doctoring for Children's Hospital, usually that is.

Sarah called us earlier than usual on a recent Sunday to tell us a story about what happened to her that morning at her church, the Oakmont Presbyterian Church, not far from her townhouse residence in Oakmont Commons.

Kathie and I were talking to her on separate telephones in our home. "I had my worst nightmare in church this morning," said Sarah.

Matt, who usually accompanies her to church on Sunday, was away, on a fishing trip. So she was there alone. During the service, an elderly gentleman seated nearby, slumped over in the pew.

The minister didn't make the usual announcement, "Is there a doctor in the house?"

No, he knew better than that. The minister, Dr. Steve Wilson, pointed directly at my daughter from his pulpit and announced instead, "Sarah's a doctor!"

Hearing that part of the story, her mother asked, "Did you want to bolt for the door?"

Sarah said, "No, I went over to him to see what was wrong. We revived him, and he was feeling better. His family thought he might have taken too much of his blood pressure medicine that morning. They called for the emergency medical service, and they took him to a hospital in an ambulance to have him checked out. He's okay."

"So you saved his life," I said, always the proud father.

"Sure, Dad, if you say so," said Dr. Sarah, always eager to please me.

"What did you do for him?" I asked.

"I put a cool damp cloth on his forehead," said Dr. Sarah, "and I gave him a glass of water to drink."

"Where'd you learn to do that?" I asked, always having to press her for more information. Neither Kathie nor Sarah surrender stories easily, unlike their husband and father, respectively.

"I learned it from you, Dad," said Dr. Sarah. "Whenever Rebecca and I weren't feeling well, you would always come into our bedrooms and put cold cloths on our foreheads, and get us a glass of water or juice. I remember it always felt so good."

Well, Sarah couldn't see me, but I was positively beaming. As a father, with Father's Day fast approaching, it felt good to hear that.

A few days later, I received a telephone call from Matt. Sarah had told us Matt was disappointed that he wasn't with her in church that day so he could've tended to the old man in distress. "She's been with Dr. Starzl and all these great doctors during her training at Pitt Medical School and her residency at Children's Hospital," said Dr. Matt, "and who does she credit for teaching her what she did that day? You!"

It was the best Father's Day gift she could have given me.

Dr. Sarah O'Brien, Dr. Thomas Starzl and Dr. Matthew Zirwas meet on roof garden outside Dr. Starzl's Oakland office. Dr. Starzl is a world-renowned transplant surgeon and research specialist.

Enjoying a holiday party
in a hospital

December 29, 2003

A road sign proclaimed Indiana, Pennsylvania, as the Christmas tree capital of the world. Later, a local woman informed me that Jimmy Stewart was from Indiana, Pa. Heck, everyone knows that.

This did bring to mind his holiday movie, *It's A Wonderful Life*, which gets shown on TV about a dozen times every December.

'Twas the week before Christmas and Indiana, Pa. seemed like the perfect place to be to get into the proper spirit for the holiday season.

Some places just lend themselves to that better than others. It was more of a mixed bag the day before when I attended a Christmas party at Allegheny General Hospital on our city's North Side.

It was the second year in a row I went there for a holiday get-together. The doctors and hospital staff have their families come in for the occasion, and toss a party for the patients and their families.

My wife is a social worker in the oncology unit. She assists patients and their families to deal with and resolve the problems that arise from such illnesses and related challenges.

Kathie likes her job, though it gets real difficult some days, especially when someone dies after a special relationship has developed during their stay at the hospital.

"It's been a difficult day," one woman doctor in the oncology unit said as she started to munch on some of the goodies she had put on her plate, "and it's hard to change faces and get into a festive party mood."

In short, her plate was already full before she entered the room where wonderful food could be found.

But the doctors and nurses and staff members were all smiling their best smiles, and the patients and their families were doing their best to do the same. The interaction was uplifting for all. It was just different from the daily routine.

There was plenty of good food and drink, and holiday treats. The kids, in particular, didn't have any difficulty in getting into the spirit of the occasion. They were bunched around the buffet table competing for cookies and brownies and all sorts of sweets.

A little boy, about six or seven years old, however, put it all in perspective when his mother was parking the car before they joined their father, a young doctor in the unit.

The little boy asked his mother what they were doing there. "We're going to a party," she said.

"No, we're not," the little boy said. "We're going to the hospital."

Hospitals are to be complimented for brightening up their buildings in recent years. I have visited family and friends at Mercy Hospital, St. Clair, Children's and Allegheny General and can appreciate the renovations many have made to modernize their facilities. Some lobbies rival that of the Vista International Hotel. Some critics complain about the posh surroundings. Hey, someone has to pay for it. Aren't medical costs high enough?

I welcome the change. It's difficult enough for patients and loved ones to spend time there.

I used to hate to go to hospitals. I hated the smells. I had major surgery as a child that required doctors and nurses to clean adhesive marks around my mouth with ether-soaked cloths. It had an awful smell.

For years, when I got a whiff of ether or anything that smelled like it. I would do a header onto the floor. I cracked my cranium a couple of times from passing out on those hard floors. You don't smell those kinds of smells in hospitals anymore.

252

I used to decline whenever my brother Dan invited me to join him in visiting a friend or relative at a hospital. That was before the late owner of the Steelers, Art Rooney Sr., educated me as to why you should go to hospitals to visit patients.

It's a good place to put your own problems into perspective. When you go to a hospital, whether you are a patient, family member or friend, you will find patients with worse problems than yours. Someone always has a bigger problem.

It makes you count your blessings for the year that has passed and offers hope for the coming year. But not for some.

At the party at Allegheny General Hospital, I saw an 18-year-old girl wearing a face mask to protect her from infection. She has leukemia.

There was a handsome young man sitting next to his girlfriend. He was wearing a cap to cover his head that had become bald from chemotherapy treatments. He had cancer, too. There was a middle-aged woman with Down's Syndrome, who lately had added leukemia to her list of problems.

A family that had come in for the party also checked with my wife about some paperwork necessary for the daughter of a patient to become a legal guardian for her father who had been diagnosed as incompetent to handle his own affairs. Such situations make it difficult for the family to get into the holiday spirit, for sure.

Christmas is a challenge for many. As I was driving down the highway through Indiana, Pa., and thinking about Jimmy Stewart, I realized what a wonderful life most of us lead, and how we have to be more concerned and involved with those who are sick and suffering.

It's a good vow to put on your list of New Year's resolutions. To care a little more. To try, anyhow.

> *"Stolen kisses are always sweetest"*
> **— Leigh Hunt**

Trying to find the perfect Valentine's Day card

February 12, 2004

I am looking for the perfect Valentine's Day greeting card. It's for my wife, Kathie, of course, and I know just what I want. I always give her a Hallmark card showing a couple of cuddly bears or bunny rabbits in several sequences. It shows them fussing over one another, feuding about something, watching TV together, snuggling and, at the end, kissing or dancing away the night.

I always draw a mustache on all the male figures, and maybe a "JOB" on his shirt or cuffs, just to make sure Kathie knows who gave her the card.

A minister was talking about love last Sunday in his sermon, and I turned to Kathie and said, "I only put up with you because I love you." She smiled. I have done my best from the beginning to put a smile on her face. She always said she married me because I made her laugh.

As I move farther into my 60s, I've become more aware and appreciative of what Kathie has contributed to my life. I see senior couples walking in the shopping malls, some holding hands, and I always am impressed when I see people who are still thrilled about one another.

We are in our 37th year together. I liked her from the first time I laid eyes on her when we were both in graduate school at Pitt, seeing her at a party in Oakland. Her beautiful brown eyes seized my blue eyes. She was attractive and smart, a wonderful combination.

She is demanding of me every day, and it wears me out sometimes, but I know she has brought order, balance and love, and two beautiful and smart daughters into our lives.

Rebecca O'Brien, general manager of California Pizza Kitchen in Tarzana, California, poses with manager Chad Franson.

Sarah and Rebecca flank their mother.

She's been a demanding, but wonderful mother. The expectations for all of us have been high. I'm grateful. She gives me direction; oh does she give me direction. But I need it.

My mother told me to stay busy and stay out of trouble, and Kathie continues to carry that torch, applying it to my backside if I appear to be slowing down or slipping. She has always appreciated the demands of my work, and was never one to complain when I had to travel, or be somewhere. She understood.

Kathie is better at being alone, and relishes solitude more than I do. She is more comfortable in her own company. When I lost a job, she had one within a few days. She never blamed me, but provided a bridge for me to do something I really dreamed of doing. She has a great work ethic, which she inherited from her family. Now I can't get her to quit. Our kids, Sarah and Rebecca, both think that their mom spoils me, and that she does too much for me. They are of a different generation, and believe that housecleaning and doing laundry should be shared work. I know I am spoiled and I like it that way, and Kathie knows she has freedoms not offered by some husbands. She doesn't have to check with me, for instance, about doing whatever she wants to do. Don't argue.

I tell young couples that two of the secrets of a successful marriage are that a husband should adore his wife, and that he should never ask what anything costs. I have only broken that latter rule once. I have asked Kathie on several occasions what Sarah's wedding cost and I still haven't gotten an answer.

Rebecca has repeatedly told me, just to boost my confidence, "Mom's the only one who'd marry you."

Maybe she's right. One of the other reasons I was attracted to Kathie was because she liked me. That doesn't mean she doesn't get under my skin sometimes. But I also tell young couples never to go to bed mad at their mate. Make up before you turn in for the night.

It's also a good idea not to run when a crisis develops in your relationship. Remember why you married in the first place. Commitment is critical to staying the course. Guys get stupid sometimes, and it's important to have someone to smarten you up. I am providing Kathie with a new challenge these days. My heels have been hurting me for sometime now, and I went to the doctor to get them checked out. My Achilles tendons are tight. The soles of my feet are often tender. One of the ways to correct this problem is that I have to wear boots at night to keep my feet properly extended. I look like a goalie in hockey when I go to bed. I tell Kathie she is sleeping with Jacque Plante. He is a Hall of Fame goaltender, the first to wear a protective mask. That might be next for me at night. Kathie laughs at the sight of me. "Do you have your boots on?" she asks when I enter the bedroom.

Our parents are gone now, and our girls are away on their own. Sundays are especially different when none of them is with us. Kathie and I need each other more than ever. I don't wait till Valentine's Day to tell her I love her. I tell her every day.

Christmas reunion: left to right, Quinn, Jim, Rebecca, Kathie, Sarah and Matt

Maggie could feel
the thunder at Pitt-UConn contest

February 18, 2004

A man was sitting next to me Sunday at the Petersen Events Center with a child sitting on his lap the entire basketball game between Pitt and Connecticut. It was his grandchild, I learned. Her name was Anaelle — not Anabelle, mind you — and she will be five years old in May. His name is Allan Press and he lives in Mt. Lebanon. I told him I was going to be a grandparent for the first time this May.

"Being a grandparent is the greatest thing in the world," he told me. "The only problem is she lives in France."

Yes, my older daughter, Dr. Sarah O'Brien-Zirwas, 30, is expecting in mid-May. I'm finally allowed to tell you. A series of sonogram tests have shown she is having a girl. She and her husband, Dr. Matthew Zirwas (pronounced Zye-russ) are going to name the baby Margaret and they will call her Maggie.

I can't wait till Maggie is big enough to sit on my lap in those same seats at a Pitt basketball game. I'm ready to be a grandfather.

Sarah was standing now and pulling for the Panthers to hold off the Huskies' late charge in a contest that more than lived up to its billing as a battle of two nationally-ranked Big East powers. I marvel at Sarah's ever-changing figure. My wife Kathie and I have season tickets in seats next to Sarah and Matt, and we love to go to the games together.

As great as grandchildren are, there's also a different joy to keeping company with your children when they become adults. We once had first-row seats at Fitzgerald Field House, the former home of the Pitt Panthers, and I remember

Matt and Sarah wear their Oakland Zoo shirts proudly as they pull for their Pitt basketball team. They enjoyed trip to New York to see Pitt play in Big East Basketball Tournament at Madison Square Garden in March of 2004.

Rebecca wears Pitt cheerleading outfit her Grandma Churchman made her for "Photo Day" session at Pitt Stadium in August of 1985.

it wasn't that long ago that Sarah was dancing with the Pitt Panther mascot during a break in the game action. When I worked in the Pitt athletic department as the sports information director in the mid-80s, Sarah and her kid sister, Rebecca, had their own blue and gold cheerleader costumes that their Grandmother Churchman made for them. Was it that long ago?

Where have my little girls gone? Rebecca recently learned that she has been promoted to general manager of her own California Pizza Kitchen Restaurant just north of Los Angeles in the San Fernando Valley. And she's going to be an aunt before she knows it.

Sarah has always been a big sports fan, and she especially loves basketball. Sarah used to accompany us when we went to New York for the Big East basketball tournament at Madison Square Garden. Rebecca stayed home with her grandparents. Matt is accompanying us this March when we're going to New York to see the tournament while the Big East still has all its traditional teams.

Sarah was on call on Sunday at Children's Hospital, just down DeSoto Street from the Petersen Events Center. She would be on call till 8 a.m. on Monday. She was paged several times during the game, and it was hard for her to talk on her cell phone because the Petersen Events Center was never noisier. Brent Musburger and Dick Vitale were telling a CBS-TV national audience what a tremendous scene it was.

When the sellout crowd was not creating a din, the Pitt pep band was blaring loud. It's great, unless you're on call at your hospital that is.

Pitt, ranked fourth in the nation just ahead of UConn, won this exciting nail-biter, 75-68. We decided to have dinner at Joe Mama's, an Italian restaurant on Forbes Avenue near Children's Hospital. No sooner were we seated than Sarah got a call and had to leave and go to the emergency room at Children's Hospital. She had to determine whether or not a certain test should be administered to an ailing child. She returned in time for the main entrée.

Sarah is in her first year as a fellow in the pediatric oncology department at Children's. It's a challenging mission.

On Saturday, I was doing a book signing at Waldenbooks at Ross Park Mall. I could hear a youth orchestra performing over a four-hour period. It reminded me of the times Kathie and I went there to hear Sarah play her cello. I learned that the group performing was the Three Rivers Young People's Orchestra. That's the same orchestra in which Sarah performed.

One of the songs they played was "Somewhere Over The Rainbow" from *The Wizard of Oz*. That's Sarah's favorite song. That's the song she and I danced to at her wedding reception nearly six years ago. I watched a parade of parents pushing babies in strollers, or carrying them in their arms, with extra attention.

I thought about Sarah and Rebecca, and how much I enjoyed pushing them in baby carriages about our neighborhood on Long Island where they were both born. And I thought about Maggie, and what she would look like. I thought that she was waiting her turn, waiting out there somewhere over the rainbow.

Mel Blount and Bill Cowher of the Steelers were among the 12,817 fans they counted coming through the turnstiles Sunday. It was a record-setting crowd. That little girl who sat next to me wasn't included in that total and neither was Maggie Zirwas. But someday she will be telling her friends that she was there when Pitt beat Connecticut for its 40th straight home court victory during the 2003-2004 season. If she's anything like her mother, that is.

> *"Marriages are made in heaven."*
> **— John Lyly**

I'm ready to be Maggie's grandpap any day now

May 5, 2004

Iam going to be grandpap for the first time soon. Any day now. My wife Kathie and I can't wait for the blessed event. Our daughter's due date is May 19. But who knows? Maybe the baby will arrive on Mother's Day.

Sarah and her husband, Matt Zirwas, have known for months that the baby will be a girl. The sonogram showed that. I think that sonogram picture would have made me squeamish when I was about to be a father. I was hoping for a girl. I'm comfortable with girls. Sarah and her sister Rebecca have brought much joy to our lives. Her parents are naming her Margaret and they are going to call her Maggie. I'm happy with that, too. Maggie is a name with some character.

Her full name will be Margaret Harvey Zirwas. That's quite a handle. Harvey is her mother's middle name. It was the first name of her great-grandfather and her great-great-grandfather. It's also the name of Sarah's uncle, who lives in North Carolina. Maggie will learn soon enough how to tell people the proper pronunciation for her last name. It's Zi-rus, as in virus.

I believe Maggie is going to be a writer. I can hardly wait to walk with her and hold her hand, or carry her across a busy street as snow is falling, the way I once did with her mother in Manhattan. Her mom and I used to go to movies together. When we'd come home, her mom used to keep track of her ten favorite movies and she'd make adjustments to her lineup, depending on how much we liked or didn't like a particular movie.

Her mom and dad are both doctors. Her mom is a fellow in pediatric hematology/oncology at Children's Hospital in Oakland, and her dad is a dermatologist next door at UPMC. Her parents are both bright. When Sarah learned she was pregnant, one of her long-time friends, Hollee Schwartz Temple, asked her in jest if Mensa had been notified of the forthcoming birth.

Her sister Rebecca has always said that Sarah and Matt enjoyed what she called "Nerd love," and asked if the baby would be a Nerdlette. That Rebecca never stops needling her older sister, or all of us for that matter. Rebecca will be 27 on May 7 and she is looking forward to being an aunt, even if long distance from southern California.

She has already made plans to fly here next month to see Maggie and her mother. Sarah is 30. Her mother Kathie turned 30 one month after Sarah was born back in 1973.

I wake up every morning, at least for the last few weeks, thinking about Sarah and Maggie. Then I think about Rebecca because if I don't think about her as much as I think about her sister she will know and I will be in trouble. They have always insisted on equal time.

My stomach has been tied up in knots for a month. You'd think I was having a baby. I have confessed to Kathie that I don't remember being this nervous when she was about to have Sarah or Rebecca. I was just overjoyed at their impending arrival.

When your wife tells you that she's pregnant you are excited. When your daughter tells you she's pregnant you start worrying. That's the difference between being 31 and 61. I want everything to go well.

Billy Crystal, the brilliant comic, has written a book about waiting to become a grandfather. It's called *I Already Know I Love You*, and it's illustrated by Elizabeth Sayles. It's a best-seller already. I have read it several times, and I gave Sarah a copy and told her to perch it on her belly and start reading it to Maggie now. Give her a head start on being smart. The book begins with these lines:

"I'm going to be a grandpa! I have the biggest smile. I have been waiting to meet you, for such a long, long while."

He also wrote lines like this: "I'm waiting to show you everything."

And "I want to feel your heart beat as you lie upon my chest."

And, "I want to show you the wind, and how it bends the grass. I waiting to give you bear hugs — the kind that last and last."

I first met Billy Crystal when I was covering the Mets and Yankees in New York back in 1972. Crystal came to a baseball writers' luncheon at Mamma Leone's in midtown Manhattan and entertained us with his imitations of Casey Stengel, who had managed both teams. Crystal was a young comic back then, just getting started, and I had been married for five years and Sarah was still a year away from being born. "I already know I love you as I sit here and wait," Crystal continues in his beautiful book. I know the feeling. Sarah is still working in the cancer clinic at Children's Hospital. I think they're just going to put her on a gurney and wheel her down to Magee Womens Hospital to have her baby. It should be exciting.

Two weeks ago I was signing autographs one morning at a Breakfast With Champions event sponsored by the Leukemia & Lymphoma Society at a downtown hotel. Three beautiful young girls came to my table together with programs to be signed. I asked them their names. One was named Olivia. The other two were named Maggie. That caught my attention. They were all so beautiful. One of the Maggies had the darkest, most magical eyes.

The other day I was doing a book signing, and my buddy Don DeBlasio came by with his new wife. Her name is Maggie, too. "It's become a real popular name," she told me. So many Maggies…

I have been checking out the little girls and babies in the shopping malls more than ever in recent months. I look at them and wonder if Maggie will look like them. Billy Crystal wrote about wanting to hug his grandchild, wanting to walk the beaches and tell the baby why the sky is blue. He wanted to show her things and teach her things. Grandparents keep telling me how wonderful it is, and that it will change my life forever. "I'm going to be your grandpa," continues Crystal, "and I can hardly wait." Maggie, take your time. Stay warm and wait till everything is just right. Be here on schedule. And, yes, I already know I love you.

Sarah and Matt were expectant parents in April of 2004.

A truly memorable Mother's Day and then some

May 12, 2004

I can't wait to tell my stories to my granddaughter. I especially want to tell her about the excitement and commotion she created on Mother's Day, 2004. Her mother knows most of my stories. Her dad knows some of them. Her grandmother knows all of them. And they were all a part of her first story.

Margaret, or Maggie as she's going to be known, missed being a Mother's Day gift by eight or nine minutes. She arrived nine days ahead of schedule. She was the first baby born on Monday at Magee Womens Hospital, but she was a bit late for the date I had set for her birth. I thought Maggie might have a touch of the theater in her. I noticed on my date calendar, however, that Monday was Mother's Day in Mexico. Maybe we ought to name her Margarita. It was still Mother's Day in California.

My wife Kathie and I kept a vigil at Magee on Sunday from eight o'clock till midnight and then went home. We had been up at six o'clock that morning and we both had to get up at the same time on Monday to start our workday. There was no word that Maggie might be arriving any time soon.

Babies don't always look their best when they are born, and I think Maggie wanted to get a bath and her make-up on before we met for the first time. Our daughter Sarah and her husband Matt had come to Oakland that morning because Sarah seemed ready to have her baby.

Kathie and I were in Oakland at the same time, but didn't know that Sarah and Matt were nearby. We were there to participate once again in the Susan B. Komen 5K

Race/Walk for Breast Cancer Research. We were walking in memory of Kathie's mother, Barbara Churchman, who had died from breast cancer two years earlier at age 83.

A record 40,000 participants showed up on a perfect Sunday morning at Schenley Park to run or stroll a little more than three-mile route. The cancer survivors wore pink T-shirts and ballcaps. Most people had signs posted on their back as to whether they were there in memory of a loved one or celebrating the life of someone who is battling breast cancer.

When I read those signs about "My Mom" or "My Aunt" or "My Best Friend," I get emotional. It just overwhelms me for a time. So many loved ones lost, so many loved ones being challenged. So much love in the park. Kathie and I wished our moms were still alive. We miss talking to them, sharing our stories. With Sarah soon to have a baby, it would have been nice for them to see their grandchild having a child of her own. That would have been special.

We saw people we knew had cancer in their pink outfits, and we saw a few people we weren't aware had cancer. The Komen Race/Walk is a coming out party of sorts for those challenged by cancer. It is a wake-up call for everybody to appreciate the importance of good health.

We saw young parents pushing babies in strollers through Schenley Park. One was just two-and-a-half-weeks old. Next year, I thought, I'll be pushing Maggie. She'll be taking someone else's place in the parade.

When we arrived at home we picked up the phone message that Matt left us, saying he and Sarah were at Magee Womens Hospital. He said nothing was imminent. He would call back and keep us posted.

We kept busy and enjoyed the day, and we had a Mother's Day dinner at Atria's Restaurant & Tavern in Peters Township. We saw friends and shared the news that we might be having a granddaughter later in the day. When I was signing books at South Hills Village on Friday, many readers of this column came by and asked, "Well, are you a grandfather yet?" Or, "Is Maggie here yet?" Or, "She's in our prayers." I felt warmed by all of this.

When we were at Magee Womens Hospital, we heard another woman wailing for a half-hour before she gave birth to her baby. But there was no noise in Sarah's room. So we went home.

We got the good news over the phone upon arrival, and wished we had stayed longer. We got to see Maggie at 11 a.m. on Monday. It was worth the wait. She is beautiful, of course. She surprised us by weighing in at a hefty 9 pounds, 1 ounce. She is 21 inches long. Sarah never seemed to appear that big during her pregnancy. Sarah was glowing and in good spirits, but understandably in some discomfort.

From the third floor at Magee, I could see Oakland Avenue a few blocks away. That's where Kathie lived when I first met and dated her. Sarah and Matt also met in Oakland, during Orientation Week at the University of Pittsburgh School of Medicine. And then Maggie is born there. Oakland is a special place in our hearts.

It was good to see her and Matt. Holding a grandchild is different from holding your own infant at birth. It's hard to explain. When you're older, I think, when you're 61 instead of 31, as I was when Sarah was born, I think you appreciate life more. I was wishing our younger daughter Rebecca was there to see her new niece. Rebecca's birthday was May 7.

I remember how I nearly fainted and pulled her mother off the gurney in the delivery room at Mercy Hospital on Long Island 27 years earlier. I was holding Kathie's hand, and I was supposed to be comforting and soothing her as she gave birth to Rebecca. Instead, Kathie was asking me if I was okay. If I had held onto her hand any longer we might have all ended up on the floor.

It's a good memory. Sarah looked like she was 15 rather than 30 as I saw her in bed the night before, as she waited to have her baby. I like to kiss Maggie on her forehead and ample cheeks and ears. She smells good. I think we're going to get along just fine, and that it's the beginning of a beautiful relationship.

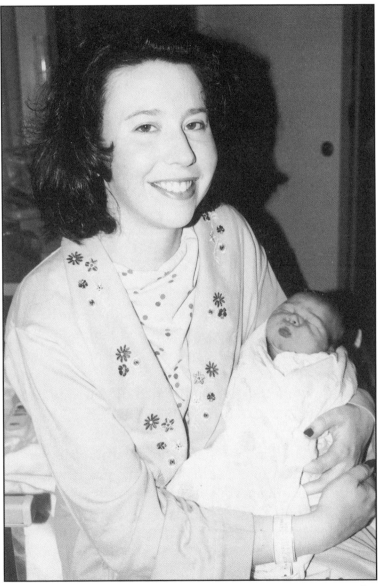

Sarah holds her daughter Margaret on her birthday, May 10, 2004, in their room at Magee Womens Hospital in Oakland.

Father's Day is different for all of us from now on

I was driving from Greensburg to Pittsburgh this past Saturday evening. When I was about 15 minutes from home, I called my wife Kathie to let her know when to expect me. I was to cook hamburgers on the outdoor grill, and she was to get everything else ready for a picnic-type dinner. I was passing Jefferson Memorial Cemetery on Lebanon Church Road. "Where are you?" she asked. I paused before I answered, and replied, "Right now . . . I am just passing your parents' gravesite."

There was a pause at the other end. "Wave to them," Kathie came back. "Hi, Mom. Hi, Dad."

She sounded almost child-like when she said that. It was such an honest response. "I wish they were coming to our home tomorrow," I said.

"I wish they were, too," she said.

We talked some more about them. We agreed that we would want them to come as they did a few years back, when they were in relatively good health and happy to greet each day, not the way they were in their last year, not when each day was so difficult for them and for us. The same could be said about my mother. My father had died within two years after we were married, back in 1969.

Kathie and I were looking forward to a Father's Day visit by our daughter Sarah and her husband Matt and their six-week-old daughter, Margaret or Maggie. It was going to be Matt's first Father's Day. It would be my first Father's Day as a grandfather.

I have a photograph I like that shows Kathie's parents and my mom, Kathie, Sarah and Matt are sitting on our back porch on a sunny day like we had this past Sunday. Everyone was well when this picture was taken. Only Margaret was missing from the picture. So it was a different scene this time.

Matt was thrilled. "I'm eight days away from finishing my residency in dermatology," he said. "I always wanted to be a doctor, be married and be a father. And I have accomplished all of these goals at age 30. I feel great about this."

It pleases me that Matt adores his daughter and my daughter so much. I also like the fact that Matt likes to talk to me, even though I am always lecturing him so much. I can't help myself. My father-in-law was a quiet, reserved man. He was a good man, but he didn't talk much. Sometimes my father talked too much. I'm more like my father.

Matt asks a lot of questions. Sarah rolls her eyes a lot when Matt asks his questions. "What advice do you have for a new father on Father's Day?" Matt asked me.

I had to think about that one for awhile. I remember when he asked me for advice about marrying Sarah. Back then, I said, "Just always adore her. And do whatever she wants to do. It's easier that way." Now I was being called upon to provide more Solomonesque advice. "Just adore Margaret's mother and always treat her right, and she will learn to respect that in a man," I said. "Just put them both first in your life. Being a doctor is a demanding career choice, but make time for Sarah and Margaret. Care about them more than you care about anyone else."

My younger daughter, Rebecca, called from California to wish me a Happy Father's Day. She is in her first months as general manager of her own restaurant and she was stressed because her restaurant is readying for a company-conducted inspection. I told her to be confident. She said she sent me a Father's Day card and thought I should have had it by now. She drew in a mustache. Sarah sent me two cards for Father's Day — one from her and Matt and one from

"Miss Margaret." She drew mustaches on a bear and a cat, and doctored up the cards like I always do. She had Miss Margaret offering me burps and toots, and said she was looking forward to seeing me on Sunday. The bear was wearing a blue denim shirt like I wear sometimes. Sarah wrote in her card: "How many dads will drive their daughter to a Big East Basketball Tournament, and to her gynecology appointment? You're A-OK, Dad." She also bought me a light blue dress shirt I liked.

Having my daughters offer positive expressions of love on Father's Day made me feel grand. Holding Margaret's warm face with those chubby cheeks against my neck made me feel like a real grandfather.

Margaret was wearing a beautiful soft yellow summer dress her Aunt Rebecca bought for her. She was also wearing a canary yellow sweater. Kathie told me it was one of three sweaters that my mother had knitted that our girls once wore. She gave them to Sarah for Margaret to wear.

During her visit to our home, Margaret took a nap in the crib that her mother and her aunt once slept in. In fact, Rebecca slept in that same crib in that same room once upon a time. Seeing Kathie holding Margaret in a rocking chair on our back porch made me realize that all of us have new roles, and we're all taking someone else's place.

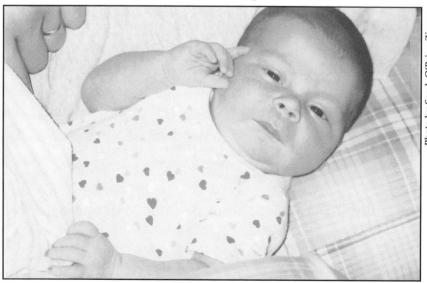

Margaret, or Maggie, made Father's Day special for everyone.